Ellen.

THE MATTER
OF LIFE
AND DEATH

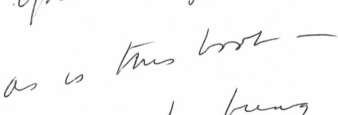

You are priceless —
as is this book —
Thanks for being
willing to laugh

for appreciation

F. T—

THE MATTER OF LIFE AND DEATH

SURVIVING LOSS AND FINDING HOPE

MSGR. THOMAS HARTMAN
WITH JOE COOK

Triumph™ Books
Liguori, Missouri

Published by Triumph™ Books
Liguori, Missouri
An Imprint of Liguori Publications

Scripture citations are taken from the *New Revised Standard Version Bible*, copyright © 1989 by the Division of Christian Education of the National Council of Churches of Christ in the U.S.A.

Library of Congress Cataloging-in-Publication Data

Hartman, Thomas.
     The matter of life and death : surviving loss and finding hope
/ Thomas Hartman, with Joe Cook.
        p. cm.
        ISBN 0-89243-639-5 : $14.95
        1. Death—Religious aspects—Catholic Church. 2. Bereave-
ment—Religious aspects—Catholic Church. 3. Future life—
Catholic Church. 4. Consolation. 5. Catholic Church—
Doctrines.   I. Cook, Joe. II. Title.
BT 825.H2863   1994
248.8'6—dc20   94-117
                                                CP

DEDICATION

For Mom, Dad, Sheila, Joanne,
Gerard, Eileen, and John.
I love you.

CONTENTS

ABOUT THIS BOOK

The Matter of Life and Death actually began some years ago when I delivered a sermon on the subject of death and dying—a courageous undertaking for a young priest. An impressed parishioner suggested I write a book on the subject of bereavement, so I started making notes and writing bits of prose that I thought might be incorporated into such a project. Although I had counseled many people in the throes of bereavement, had celebrated funeral Masses as a regular part of my ministry, and had witnessed the many faces of death, I still felt I had to know more, to witness more, to examine more closely, the emotional and physical aspects of bereavement. I needed to look more closely at death itself, at the spoken and unspoken fears of the people for whom I was offering help. The mystery of death is not a simple matter.

Over the years, I asked innumerable people how they perceived death, and the answers varied. Some showed bone-chilling fear. Others accepted the inevitability rather calmly. I discovered that the closer people were to God, the less they feared death.

But it was in the area of bereavement that people seemed to need the most counseling. Many found the loss of a loved one devastating, their lives turned upside down. Some experienced loss quietly, but carried deep wounds that would not easily heal. Others understood that death is not the end, that it is only a change. Ministering to the dying was vital, of course, but often there was an urgent need to comfort, advise, and be of help to those who mourned. It was obvious in many cases that the real burden, the real fear is, to be left behind.

In time I had a plethora of material based on my encounters with the bereaved, material that needed organization and a swift writing hand. I called upon a good friend, Joe Cook, who is an award-winning professional with an enviable background in television, radio, and books. Joe and I went over twenty years of notes and writings. Our roles were priest and scribe, and we have put together a work that, for both of us, has been a therapeutic exercise.

It is our hope that you will find this book a source of hope and faith.

Msgr. Thomas Hartman

INTRODUCTION

I had known Evelyn and Don during all their twenty-six married years. They were a delightful couple with two children, a boy, nineteen, in college, and a girl, sixteen, still in high school. They were living the American Dream. Don was now a full vice president of his financial institution on Long Island; Ev worked part time as a broadcast news consultant. The kids were doing well in school, and the future looked very bright.

When Evelyn heard the phone ring at two-thirty one afternoon, something told her that it was either Don or something about Don. She felt a slight chill when she lifted the receiver, but shrugged it off as just "nerves." When she heard the voice of Lynn Herzog, Don's secretary, she felt an appalling dread.

"I don't know how to tell you this, Mrs. Mancini, but—but your husband seemed, well...ill...and they just took him to the hospital in an ambulance."

"Heart?"

"I don't know, but they seemed to think so. But I can't be sure. I don't really know."

"Where did they take him?"

"To Saint Francis. Two of the men went with him."

"Thank you, Lynn."

"Mrs. Mancini, if there's anything I can do—anything at all…"

"Thank you, Lynn. I'll let you know."

By the time Ev called me, she was in panic and tears. I told her to get someone to drive her to Saint Francis Hospital, and I would meet her there.

Ev was waiting for me in the hospital parking lot. "Over here, Father," she called as I parked my car.

I checked with the triage nurse at the emergency admissions desk and learned, without Ev hearing, that Don had been rushed to the coronary unit upon arrival at the hospital, and he was under treatment at that very moment.

Ev and I waited for about a half hour before a staff doctor appeared with the news. Don had been declared dead on arrival at the hospital. Every device known to the staff had been used to try to resuscitate him, but it was useless. Don was gone.

From that moment on, Ev's life would change forever. She was in shock. She didn't—couldn't—believe this had happened. It was all a bad dream. I tried to comfort her with words I doubt she really heard. The greatest contribution I could make at that point was just to be there for her. We had to deal with the situation. Who to call first? What about the kids? The funeral arrangements? The church? The future? Her face told *the story. Ev was certainly in shock. Her worst possible nightmare was being played out.*

In a short while, a nagging feeling of guilt hit her. She knew that Don had been diagnosed as having a case of rather severe hypertension. A heart attack or a stroke was a possibility, if not a probability. Should she have insisted Don cut down on his work load? Should she have insisted on more tests? Should she have made another doctor's appointment, despite Don's insistence that he felt "fine"?

In the ensuing days and weeks, Ev would wonder how she would ever get through Don's passing. She would experience acute anxiety, depression, and loneliness, and the physical symptoms of stress would become apparent. She would feel anger, and feel a need to idealize Don. She would have to rely on friends—and time—before any hope for a normal life could return.

The specter of death wears many mantles. The scenarios vary, but the shock and mystery remain. As a priest and pastoral caregiver, I have been close to death hundreds—thousands—of times. My acquaintance with this earthly phenomenon began early and has proliferated over the passing years. A death in the family invites trauma, no matter how it comes, but it can also result in compassion, understanding, and deeper faith.

Death has many ramifications. Death means change; death induces fear, guilt, a sense of abandonment. Ev's story isn't unusual. What she expressed and felt is very normal. Her hope of recovery will be dependent on her ability to understand bereavement, live through it, and see it as an important part of life—but not the *only* part of her new life.

You may be grieving, or you may harbor a secret fear of your own death. Don't worry. Everybody does. If we can look at the question of death together, I believe that we can put life and death into a better perspective.

The very word *death* has a frightening, eerie, hushed undertone. No lexicographer has come up with a better word. We might say someone has "passed away" or "passed on" rather than "died"— but passed on to where? To what place? Webster calls death "the permanent cessation of all vital functions." Pretty stark stuff. But, as the story of Evelyn shows, we can't be totally clinical about death, because there is too much emotion, and too many people are involved. Death affects so much of our thinking, touches on so many individual lives, involves so much that is spiritual, that it takes on a magnitude of its own.

No two deaths are exactly alike, nor could they be. Some people actually contribute to their own deaths. Some are caught in freak accidents or by sudden viral attacks. Others suffer a lingering death with the full knowledge that their condition is terminal. We are all vulnerable. We are born, we live—and we all die. This is a given. There is no changing it.

But by exploring death more fully, perhaps we can understand it better.

1

THROUGH A CHILD'S EYES

What little education we receive on the subject of death begins almost simultaneously with our curiosity about life. Little minds find the specter of death awesome. Children are extremely curious about "real" death as opposed to the death they hear about in the tales by the Brothers Grimm who put Snow White into a deathlike sleep, but had her awakened by "love's first kiss." Children are attracted to "spooky" stories of quiet, romantic dramas that depict violent death; to stories of quiet, romantic death, such as that of Beth in *Little Women*. They laugh nervously at films that deal with vampires, the walking dead, and villains who cannot be killed. Such are the forms of fiction settling into the fertile minds of the very young.

My first recollection of an encounter with the

matter of death came when I was about five years old. My father borrowed a few dozen chairs for a family party from a friend who was a mortician. The undertaker was happy to lend my father the chairs; all we had to do was pick them up at the funeral parlor. My father asked me to come along and help him load them into the car.

A funeral parlor! I had never been to one. Would I have to go in? Would I see a dead person? (I was terrified that I might.) I had visions of a corpse suddenly sitting up in a casket. What would I do? My eyes narrowed to slits so I could close them if my nightmare occurred. The chairs couldn't be loaded into the car fast enough. Even though we were outside, I kept looking over my shoulder.

In the car on the way home, I told my dad of the fear that crept over me. He listened with, as I remember, some bemusement, and explained that everybody will die someday, and that funeral parlors are places where friends can go to see somebody they love before the deceased is brought to the church for Mass and burial at the cemetery. He told me my fears and reactions were normal for someone my age, and that many people feel uncomfortable going to a funeral home. Death, to me at that time, meant a corpse. It never occurred to me that it was a family loss, a passing on. It was just a corpse. That was it, and it was scary.

Death became more personal when I reached the third grade. I became rather taken with a classmate named Catherine, an ebullient young girl with burnished brown hair and a quick smile. I recall her walking with quick long strides. She was very popular with the girls—and the boys. Although third grade was a little early for boy-girl relationships, the boys in class thought she was quite something.

During the course of that school year, I noticed Catherine getting paler. At first, I thought it was only my imagination, but she began missing classes more often. In time we began each school day with a prayer for her. I fully expected she would get better. Once or twice I visited her house to talk about homework. One day a class assignment was to write a "get well soon" letter to Catherine.

Then one beautiful spring morning, our teacher announced softly that Catherine had died in her sleep. We had no idea how something in the blood could cause anyone to die, but Catherine was gone.

My first experience in a funeral parlor now returned to mind. I didn't want to go. It was not only the fear of the mortuary itself, but I was afraid to see what Catherine looked like in death. Would she look like she was asleep? Would she be even paler than I remembered? I wondered how she must have felt when she died. These questions filled my mind, and as I put on my best suit, I felt queasy and my palms were sweaty. What would I say if anyone spoke to me?

My folks drove me to the funeral parlor where my classmates were assembled outside to enter as a group at a prearranged time. When I saw my friends, some of the fear left me. They were all as uneasy as I was.

When we entered the room where the wake was being held, the effect was more calming than I had anticipated. The room was brightly lit. There were cheerful, actually happy faces and warm conversation was being shared. Catherine lay in a beautiful casket at the front of the room. Her parents seemed happy to see us, and although there were some tears, they seemed to be quickly wiped away.

Then came the moment I dreaded—looking down at Catherine. She was surrounded by flowers. She wore a white dress, I remember, and rosary beads had been placed in her hands. She seemed to be sleeping quietly, with a very slight smile on her face. I suddenly realized that I had never seen Catherine with her eyes closed.

Another classmate and I stopped at the open casket to say some Hail Marys, and then I walked to the back of the room. The aroma of fresh flowers was overwhelming. All around me, adults were conversing—and not about Catherine, but talking about business, other relatives, and household problems. A subdued cacophony of sounds. I heard a few say, "I'm sorry" or "What a lovely child." Overall, the experience was quieter and somewhat more civilized and ordinary than I had expected. I felt actual disappointment.

So this is a wake, I thought. *I'll live through it, but I will always think about Catherine if I ever attend another.*

Over the years I've come to know that most children have similar anxieties about the death ritual. In some circumstances it can be more traumatic than mine.

I was telling the story of Catherine to a friend of mine who, he said, carried an aversion toward funerals all his life. As a mature, older man he still cannot handle the smell of flowers in a funeral setting. His story is worth telling here.

He was nine years old when he first became aware of his mother's illness. He was certain she would be better soon, because everyone he knew got sick and got over it. His father worked on the railroad in the Midwest in those economically perilous days, and never afforded himself the luxury of being late or missing a day's pay. My friend's siblings had grown up and gone—his nearest brother in age was ten years his senior.

So that summer of his ninth year he often spent entire afternoons chatting with his mother as she sat in her rocker looking out the bay window of the front room of their home in Wisconsin and commenting on the comings and goings of the people in the neighborhood. Occasionally his mother would ask him to turn on the radio, but after a while the sound seemed to irritate her and she preferred the peace and quiet. When she would have a seizure, she would ask the boy to leave the room. He was heartsick because he couldn't do something to relieve his mother's pain.

She would urge him to go out and play with his friends, and he often did, but even while he was playing duck on a rock or baseball in the vacant lot, he would wonder how his mother was faring.

Things seemed easier when his dad came home from work every day at four-thirty. On weekends he seemed less concerned with the possibility that his mother might not recover; his dad was there.

In time he began to notice something else. His brothers and sister, who visited quite irregularly, seemed to be around the house a lot more. People from the neighborhood whom he seldom saw began making calls, bringing cakes and pies and hot dishes.

It was his sister who paralyzed the boy one evening by stating quite unemotionally, it seemed to him, that their mother had cancer and had only a short time to live.

Why my mother? How could this happen? He knew she wasn't feeling well, but the idea of her dying...it just wasn't fair. Except for the short declaration by his sister, this is all he knew of the situation.

Relatives and strangers began to arrive more frequently. They were uncharacteristically pleasant to him, which actually added to his anxiety over what exactly was going on.

In his mother's final days, chairs were arranged in the dining room, which was separated from the downstairs bedroom by two curtains drawn back so that visitors might have a view of his mother lying in the bed. It was an old-fashioned deathwatch, and the boy found it not only intrusive but outright obscene.

During this curious watch, my friend's father took him downtown and bought him his first suit with long pants. He later realized that this is what he would wear to the funeral.

When they returned home, his sister insisted that he show their mother the new suit and stood him on a chair next to her bed. He could only look down on the agonizing form of his mother—and cry. "Why didn't you say something?" his sister later asked. He replied, "I tried to, but she didn't recognize me."

Further trauma followed when my friend was taken to the lower depths of the funeral parlor to select a casket. He would have no say, of course. This was for big people because it involved a great deal of money for the family, and money in those days was very tight. He learned from the conversation that his mother had no insurance, so a compromise had to be made regarding the quality of the casket. Some were elegant and burnished, others were dull and gray. The ones he felt were acceptable were too expensive. His father settled on a simple one, and the funeral director went to great lengths to point out its "advantages." The boy didn't like it. He felt it wasn't worthy of his mother.

As the undertaker demonstrated how the lid opened and closed, a chill went through the boy's body. He pictured his mother lying in the casket and some stranger closing the lid. He presumed that would be done at the end of the funeral rites, and resolved that he would turn around at that moment and not watch it happen. He knew she would not be breathing, but he was sure *he* would feel a terrible sense of suffocation.

A third jolt occurred when the mortician ushered the family to the room of repose where his mother lay as if sleeping on a narrow cot. She looked different to him. "We're not quite finished," the mortician said, "but she will be beautiful." When his father leaned down to kiss his mother's cheek, his sister let out a gasp of sheer horror.

Two days later, the chapel in the funeral home was packed. The boy wondered who all the people were. He was amazed that so many came to pay their last respects. Unknown to the boy, the lingering death became sorrowful news throughout the little city and, although many people didn't know the woman all that well, the story of the boy who was losing his mother became a topic of conversation.

Then came the moment he feared. Two funeral directors walked briskly to the casket as the mourners filed out. They would lower the lid as the pall bearers stood by. The boy turned away only to face an aunt he hardly knew. The aunt took him by the shoulders and spun him around. He saw them close his mother in.

At the gravesite, the first open grave he had ever seen, the mound of red clay was covered by a sheet of artificial grass. As the graveside service began, the boy could bear no more. He ran to the cars parked along the winding lane and waited for his father.

Back at the house, the kitchen table was laden with all kinds of food brought in by neighbors—casserole dishes of all kinds, pies and cakes, homemade bread, jellies and jams. "Eat," they insisted. "How do you expect to be a grown up big man if you don't eat?"

There was more confusion as the days went by. His brothers arrived one by one, impounding and carrying out pieces of furniture, jewelry—what little there was—and just about anything that could be carried. His father watched in dismay, his face showing the weariness of the past few days, but did nothing to stop them. His father worried about how he would pay the mortician, and none of his siblings or relatives offered to help share the medical or funeral expenses.

Those were the days when many families tended to ignore the feelings of a child, even at a time of bereavement. This may have been a holdover from the Victorian days when children were to be seen and not heard.

Early in the scenario just described, the father, the sister, some responsible member of the family, a friend, or a member of the clergy should have been assigned to talk with the boy and let him know it was all right to be angry, to express disbelief, to share the pain and even the guilt he might be feeling. The child should have been accepted as a part of the family rather than "just the baby." His questions should have been answered, and he should have been encouraged to express his feelings, whatever they may have been. As it was, he was isolated, cut off from a series of events that affected him very deeply. He should have been able to explore his own feelings and let them be known to someone who cared. The adults should have been aware of the fact that children know more about what's going on than their elders suspect.

Whoever should have been concerned with the boy's mental state should have been able to reassure him that his mother's death was not his fault, that his mother loved him, and she would be loved by God.

But it didn't happen, and this series of experiences made my friend a young cynic. It took him many years to overcome the feeling that the deathwatch, the wake, the funeral, were simply self-serving rites of the living. It took him many years to restore his faith in the belief that there is something after life.

Although I never suffered the trauma that my friend suffered in his early bout with the lessons of death, I do recall a time when I could look at death more philosophically. During my high school days, I rode the bus to school with a classmate named Paul, a bright, handsome young man from a very wealthy family. He was extremely well-read, and we talked about many serious matters during our daily trips.

When I was playing basketball, Paul could be found in the library. He preferred to be on the court himself, but Paul had hemophilia, a blood disease that kept him entirely out of sports. It didn't, however, keep him from being our team's greatest fan.

Paul began missing classes during his sophomore year. Academically, these absences didn't affect his good grades. Studying at home, he pulled high marks in every subject.

The summer following our sophormore year seemed to go better for Paul than had been expected. He spent a short time in the hospital, but was able to take vacation trips and keep up with the world through his voracious appetite for books and newspapers.

In the fall we returned to classes to find that a two-way telephone system had been installed so Paul could stay at home and still listen to what went on in class. He was able to talk to us and answer questions, but we noticed a frailty in his voice. I often wondered if Paul would ever return to class.

As days turned into weeks and weeks turned

into months, Paul was less able to even listen. He faced more tests, more doctors, longer hospital stays. Finally, our class professor told us that Paul's death was a distinct possibility.

This was my first experience in actual *bereavement*. My friend was dying. I didn't know what to say or do. I wanted to see Paul, but I didn't have a car, I didn't know exactly where he lived, or even if I found his address whether I would be welcome. I had heard that no one was allowed to see him.

Well, I *could* pray for him.

In the chapel, kneeling in prayer, I spoke to God. He heard my helplessness.

Paul died that year. We were told that in the last few weeks of his life Paul displayed the type of courage that could only come from faith. Doctors marveled at him. His family was proud of him. We spoke of him almost daily in class. At the wake we huddled just the way the adults had huddled at Catherine's wake. We were greeted by the family who appreciated our interest. They had done their best medically and personally—and we had done our best at a distance. His parents looked tired and drawn. They had fought a fierce battle for Paul and had lost.

The realization then hit me that all the money in the world cannot save a life.

After the funeral, I seldom saw Paul's parents. But I wondered how Paul's death might have changed them. Did they believe in life after death? Did they regret anything about their life with him? Did they feel blessed by the quality of life that their money made possible for him? Would they now donate their time and energy to help other parents who were in the situation they had weathered?

Paul's death made me a more serious thinker. I became more aware of my own frailty. There were more goals in life than achieving good grades. And I was beginning to question life.

2

CHANGING THE FACE OF DEATH

Paul and I had attended a high school seminary on Long Island, and it was there I found a mentor who would cause a tremendous change in the way I viewed death. Outstanding in that bastion of serious academia was an elderly, refined, graying gentleman named William Nagle. In our minds, however, he didn't possess a first name. He was never called anything but Mr. Nagle.

After a distinguished career in an assortment of schools, Mr. Nagle retired, but putting away the books was not for him. He had decided to spend his remaining days helping young men prepare for the priesthood.

While I can't recall his ever conducting a formal class, Mr. Nagle's presence was ubiquitous. He was anywhere he was needed. He cooked for us, recorded grades, collected book money, comforted us, and prayed for us. Most of all, he challenged us and tutored us. He was never too busy to hear us, or to help us. To me, this grandfatherly man knew more about life and living than anyone I had ever encountered. He would be, I thought then, my nomination for sainthood.

I left that high school to study at Our Lady of Angels Seminary in Albany and took with me many of the ideologies Mr. Nagle had shared with me. I thought of him often, particularly when the academic going got tough. Distance didn't dim my admiration for this man.

In those days seminarians rarely subscribed to newspapers, so it was only by the sheerest chance that I found myself paging through the local daily. And I never read the obituaries, except this one time. There it was. The notice of Mr. Nagle's death.

Now embedded in college philosophy, I still hadn't fully discarded my childhood ignorance. The announcement of Mr. Nagle's death stunned me. I felt a true physical pain deep inside. I tore the obituary out of the paper and stuffed it in my pocket. I was turning in anger against God. Why Mr. Nagle? He was so good!

With the newspaper item crumpled in a ball in my pocket, I defiantly climbed the seminary chapel stairs and descended onto a kneeler in a back pew. It was a whisper, probably, but in my brain it was a scream. *Why this death? Why this inequality? Why this injustice?* It was total ventilation—and it was against God. When the fury of emotion subsided I fell silent for some time.

Then, something happened that I will never forget. I was lifted out of my body into the presence of God. It wasn't visual or verbal. It was a feeling, a deep feeling of being in the presence of the most loving being I had ever encountered. It was a sensation of being loved—loved unconditionally. The only way I can describe it is to relate it to the sensation I feel when I'm with someone I really love, only magnified a hundred times. I felt so affirmed that there was no question this was a golden moment that would mark my life. A mysterious warmth enfolded me.

The Lord had already spoken to Moses on Mt. Sinai when others below him were doubting God's presence. Was I being invited to a special revelation to be able to say something to a cynical world that wondered whether God's love would be there at the end of life?

I sat back in the pew and reflected. I had been lifted out of myself. The experience had not been a visual one; I never pictured my Lord. But I had been acutely aware of His overwhelming presence. It freed me. I was helped and I was resolved. In that short time I had come so close, and so much had been revealed to me. Even as I write these words, I feel again the power of His presence, a sensation magnified a thousand times stronger than any previous encounter with anyone.

From that moment on my approach to death changed. Death wore a different face.

Ever since my childhood, when I had been taught that we don't live for this world but for the next, I could say that I believed in a Heaven. But that belief was only theoretical. I believed it only because others before me believed it. It was only theoretical in the passing of Catherine, but by the time Paul died, my perception of life was deeper and my prayer life more developed. I believed that meaning could come from Paul's death. That my faith became stronger with the death of Mr. Nagle was academic.

I believe that I have experienced the presence of God more than once. I have heard from many others, from circles other than religious—clerks, doctors, laborers, office workers, presidents of great companies, artists, and writers—that they, too, have had similar experiences. Most of them have drawn the same conclusion: "There's someone there."

Albert Einstein felt the presence of God. He said, "The most beautiful thing we can experience is the mysterious. It is the source of all true art and science. God is subtle, but He is not malicious. We should take care not to make the intellect our god. Intellect has powerful muscles, but no personality. Only God is God."

After that experience in the seminary chapel, I really began to trust God, to believe in His love, and to profess more openly a belief in life after death. I became more open in the matter of my own death and found myself actually drawn toward comforting others when death was in sight.

However, this newfound openness would not be tested for a while. In the late 1960s, a seminary was still an isolated place in many ways. We ventured off the grounds on occasion, and did have apostolic work to do, but for the most part, life in the seminary was devoted to studying theology, developing a prayer life, and forming good relationships with those around us.

A challenge came during those years—a challenge that afforded me an opportunity to test my newfound openness to death, while venturing away—with permission—from the isolation of the seminary. A renowned psychiatrist, Dr. Alan Kraft, invited twenty-two seminarians, two ministers, and a fellow psychiatrist to enter a course on counseling the dying at the Albany Medical Center in New York. The invitation fascinated me, and I accepted immediately. It proved to be one of the most challenging courses I have ever taken.

Each week, the group would meet in Dr. Kraft's office at the Center. He would have surveyed the hospital the previous week to discover a patient who was both very ill and willing to help future priests learn to listen. He would tell us a little bit about the patient—age, statistics of the disease, background, reaction to hospitalization and, sometimes, the prognosis. After absorbing this data, one of us would be selected to invite the patient into a special room for an interview. Speaking freely with the patient, the interviewer was expected to ask about the family and how they were reacting to the patient's condition, find out how the patient felt about his or her illness, discuss the prognosis, and ask if he or she had any unresolved questions. The format sounded simple, but the experience was very difficult.

The interviews were conducted in a good-sized area in the medical center, which allowed us space to sit in a random circle. Class participants took notes on the way each seminarian or minister conducted the interview. It was a live "performance" with twenty-five critics and Dr. Kraft paying close attention to every question, reaction, and nuance.

The interviewer for a given day would go to the patient's room and have him or her escorted to the interview room. At the end of a forty-five-minute chat, the interviewer would return the patient to his or her quarters and return to the room for the critique. This kind of exercise was extremely helpful. The "work" of each student was subject to immediate criticism and, very likely, embarrassment.

I distinctly remember my interview—and embarrassment.

"Hello, Mr. Stanton, how are you? First stay in the hospital?

"What seems to be your problem? Heart attack.

"Oh, your second one?

"How long did it take you to recover from the first one? Well, they have better medication now.

"Are you worried about your job in any way?

"How's your wife doing?

"When I was in your room I noticed that someone had sent you flowers. Your daughter? How nice of her!

"They say if you get a lot of rest, you'll be going back to work soon..."

The longer the interview continued, the dumber my questions seemed to get. I wanted to hide. I just wasn't connecting, although the patient was understanding and kind because Dr. Kraft had told him exactly what was going on. In fact, Mr. Stanton was actually trying to help me along. He would not be the typical patient of the future when I would be there as a visiting priest to help make any patient comfortable and to raise his spirits.

In this deeply moving series of exercises we discovered that we were all uncomfortable talking with the dying. We could pass the time with a few pleasantries, but when it came to the bottom line, we really didn't want to talk about death. We were to learn that it was natural to avoid it, even though in the priesthood days to come we would face death almost daily. It was not at all fearful to read about it, to hear about it, to discuss it. But it was another matter to talk about it with somebody who was terminally ill.

In reviewing my own interview, I felt that I was

encouraging, pleasant, even gregarious; but in his critique, Dr. Kraft asked me if I really believed that Mr. Stanton could easily accept his heart disease. Did I really believe he was sleeping well at night? Hadn't I realized that Mr. Stanton could lose his job or, worse, never be able to return to work at all—or the worse possible scenario—that Mr. Stanton may never leave the hospital alive? Did I ask about, or show any concern for, his family and what adjustments they were making? And where was God? Did Mr. Stanton believe in God? Did he want to talk about his belief? Did he question eternal life?

Dr. Kraft's review was accurate. I didn't feel comfortable with death. Something was missing that books hadn't given me. He saw my pain and said, "Tom, in order to help someone else face his death, you have to be willing to face your own death. You have to define what you believe about life and death. Until you can contemplate your own death, you won't be able to help anyone who is dying."

I was young, so although I certainly had considered it, I never faced it.

Except for the isolated times I've described, my own death was seldom in the forefront of my thoughts. On the occasions when I did think about it, I found the subject of my own death rather awesome, frightening, and "unreal." Often it would vanish in a moment, but other times it would stay with me for a while, making me quite uncomfortable.

There is a myth that young people consider

themselves immortal. It certainly may seem that way
to worried adults who see young people exhibit
questionable eating habits, take life-threatening
chances, smoke and drink to be accepted by peers,
and lane-jump at excessive speeds through heavy
traffic—giving no thought to their own eventual
death.

Fortunately, these attitudes are not universally
true. Young people do start considering their own
ends from the moment they first learn about death.
To the young, living dangerously is a "show-off"
thing. In talking with hundreds of young people, I
find that most of them do, from time to time,
contemplate their own deaths, however briefly. They
learn what death is when one of their classmates is
taken from them, when a grandparent dies, or when
they lose a pet. They perceive death from a reaction
of their parents and relatives, and often sense the
pain and sorrow that others feel.

Interestingly enough, small children may
become somewhat imured to violence and death by
the seemingly innocent traditional stories in fairy
tale books that are read to them, by what they behold
in children's "classics," and by what they see on
television. Terrible things happen to heroes and
heroines, ogres and trolls, wicked kings and queens
in Mother Goose stories and the Brothers Grimm,
whose stories are still immensely popular but remain
very grim. The Grimm brothers were entranced
with young women who were forever at death's door.

The Grimm stories, Mother Goose tales, and other fables have been appropriated over the years by modern storytellers—Walt Disney being a good example, with his screen versions of *Snow White and the Seven Dwarfs, Bambi,* and *Sleeping Beauty.*

There is something very interesting in the concept of these three stories and many more like them. The favorite plot of the Grimm brothers focused on death and resurrection. In *Snow White* we have a young woman who has lost her father—a king, at that—and is forced to scrub the floors and steps of her own castle under the watchful eye of a cruel stepmother who is jealous of her beauty. So the girl runs away. A woodsman who is ordered to murder the girl begs her to flee. She runs through the woods until she finds a safe haven in a small cottage, the home of seven dwarfs—an example of how even the meek and disabled can help overcome adversity and turn love and kindness into a strength that will overcome all. When the queen turns herself into a witch, she poisons an apple and sets out as a beggar woman to find Snow White and do her in. Snow White, showing compassion for a sweet old peddler-lady, takes the apple, bites into it, and "dies."

But what the reader or viewer knows is that Snow White will live again when she receives "love's first kiss." Earlier in the story, we learn that a prince has seen Snow White and is smitten by her beauty, but then loses track of her. Meanwhile, the dwarfs find Snow White so beautiful, even in death, that they can't find it in their hearts to bury her, so they fashion a casket of gold and glass and stand vigil by her side. Soon the prince arrives, lifts the casket lid and kisses Snow White, who, of course, awakens from her deathlike sleep. He lifts her out of her casket and carries her to his own kingdom where, naturally, they live happily ever after.

In some versions of this tale, the queen is subsequently stoned to death or beheaded, but more recent tellings spare children this epilogue.

When Bambi's mother is shot as "man comes into the forest," the young fawn realizes he has to fend for himself and learn the hard lessons of life. Bambi's reward, of course, is that after he overcomes his bereavement and is ready to face the world again, he is now the brave proud stag that stands atop the hill. He is the master of all the deer in the forest, and we see him contemplate his kingdom.

Augment this with all the fictional killing children are exposed to on television, consider their exposure to the plethora of newscasts, and there is no doubt that children find death interesting, if not traumatic.

Children may be either fascinated by death or repelled by it. Adults must understand that children don't have the vocabulary to express the way they are feeling. Their life experience has given them little understanding of what is happening to them. "Why did Rover die? What was the matter with him? Is he in Heaven? Was it my fault? Will Grandpa ever come to see us again? Why not?"

It's important for adults to understand they play a crucial role in the future lives of children—what they think, how they think, what worries them, and what scares them. When adults fail to respond to a child's questions, or when a child feels insecure, grief and wounds can be carried into adulthood. These are manifested in later life as fear of being left alone, fear of the dark, a loathing of wakes and funerals, and so on.

By and large, young people know death vicariously. Grieving is something other people do. They understand bereavement, they understand loss and despair, but as long as it isn't an imminent thing for them, they are easily distracted from this form of introspection.

This is not to say that young people never think about their own death. I've counseled teenagers who have found themselves in a state of great anxiety worrying about death. Generally, they or someone close to them are suffering some ailment that, to them, seems life-threatening. Others have witnessed the death of someone they knew very well and gone into a depression by association. Some suffer a form of panic when they realize that they, like everyone else, are merely mortal.

I was visiting a family whose teenage son had recently experienced the shock of the death of one of his close friends. A group of young people from his school had taken a vacation trip to the Bahamas.

While there, they went to party on what they called a "drunk boat." In the course of the evening, one of the boys, a popular kid who was a baseball star, drifted away from the crowd to the aft of the boat. There was a scream from one of the girls as the boy's bloodied body bobbed to the surface. He had fallen or was pushed overboard, and although someone had yelled "Man overboard!" the boy had been caught by the rotary blades of the boat.

Suddenly, there was a conspiracy of silence surrounding his death. Some parents thought it was related to the question of whether he fell, in a drunken state, or was pushed overboard as a lark. I discussed this so-called conspiracy with the parents of one of the youngsters who was on deck that fateful night. The mystery of how the boy met his death was a possibility, they thought, but more than likely the silence came from a sort of collective guilt and facing up to the reality that one of their friends was actually dead.

I live in the upper reaches of Holy Trinity High School on Long Island. All through the school year, I see and am aware of the comings and goings of hundreds of high school students. Whenever a classmate dies—as infrequently as it is—I notice a tremendous ripple effect on all the kids. There is a quiet that indicates both shock and introspection. Suddenly their peer was not immortal after all. Situations like this call for a sensitive school administration—and the availability of counselors.

In one instance, some months after the death of a popular student, the teacher was going through a stack of name cards. When she came to the name of the deceased, she unthinkingly tore the card into bits and dropped it in the wastebasket near her desk. It was enough to cause one girl in the class to cry out "Oh, my God!" and burst into tears.

For young people there is a great need to talk about the deceased. Most children face the mystery of death when a pet dies or is "put to sleep." And again, it might be the death of a grandparent, or an aunt or uncle.

When children reach adolescence they tend to become philosophical. They start raising questions: *Who am I? Why am I here? Where am I going? What's going to become of me?* These questions are stored in a young person's mind. Generally, young people have only their own life experiences to go by. A teenager looks at the death of his father. He is sixteen, his father a comparatively young forty-six. He thinks: *My father grew up, became a banker, had a family—and died. Is that it?*

Almost inevitably this youngster's grades will go down; his interest in his family will diminish. He might even drift into some habits that are anti-social. Maybe alcohol or drugs.

This is the time when an adolescent needs to be heard. There is a great need to talk about the deceased, perhaps even a need for counseling. There are many crises in a young person's life, probably more than an adult—even a parent—would understand, death of a family member or friend being not the least among them.

So parents should make a point of bringing the young person into the fold. If the parents find that they don't know what to say, there is the priest, the minister, the rabbi—and, of course, there is the therapist.

It is very easy to ignore a young person's place in the family. The more parents think of their offspring as people and not just kids, the easier the adjustment to difficult times. Let them know it's all right to grieve, that there is more to life than merely existing and dying.

3

THE STAGES
OF DYING

During my seminary training, I had the good fortune of being able to attend a few lectures by Dr. Elisabeth Kübler-Ross, a woman who practiced general medicine in Switzerland before coming to the United States where she began her work with the dying while teaching psychiatry at the University of Chicago. What impressed me most about Dr. Kübler-Ross was her ability to zero in on the problems involved in accepting the end of life on earth, and her excellent approach in answering the questions of professional people, the clergy, the media, and families who are faced with the care of the dying.

Dr. Kübler-Ross points out that the dying patient passes through certain specific stages of his or her struggle to come to grips with illness and ultimate death. These are:

- *Shock/Denial*
- *Anger*
- *Bargaining*
- *Depression*
- *Acceptance*

In the *shock* and *denial* stage, the patient experiences internal reactions, such as dizziness, numbness, possibly nausea. These symptoms can last from a few moments to the duration of the patient's life.

Denial is a little more complicated than shock. It comes in many forms. The patient argues that the diagnosis is "incorrect," that there is "no illness" at all. *The road ahead is a long one, full of good health and happiness. Doctors make mistakes, are overcautious, and are interested only in treatment and money.* Such a patient may make unrealistic long-range plans, even disobeying the doctor's orders.

Denial comes and goes. One day the patient will be certain there is a mistake; on the next day, he is certain that he is a "goner." However, denial is not necessarily a bad thing. Denial is a very essential mechanism. It helps allay the fearful thoughts that are morbid, depressing, and frightening. Without denial the patient would think only of pain, breathlessness, incapacitation, being a burden to himself and others, and withering away.

But by the same token, utter denial can possibly set up barriers between the patients, family members, and the doctors. There will come a time when it is necessary to break through the denial barriers so that sharing can take place. It is extremely difficult for most terminally ill patients to begin sharing immediately, because they are entering the second stage—*anger*.

This is when the patient says, "Oh, no! Not me!" And then she asks the biggest question of all, the one that concerns her very faith. *Why me?* The patient is resentful, bitter, and very angry. She becomes irritable and difficult to handle. She will look at an apparently healthy person and wonder, silently, *Who's letting you live? Why hasn't God done this to you? What did I ever do to deserve this?*

Anger may first alarm the family, because seldom will the patient actually say that he is angry about being sick. Rather, he will direct the anger at doctors, nurses, the food he's given, the tests he's taking, and even loved ones. There is nothing much a spouse, relative, or friend can do to stop this reaction, because anger is a spontaneous human feeling and should be allowed to come out. It's generally believed that to frustrate this outpouring of anger is to push the patient into a manic situation that will only make things worse.

I have seen this kind of anger in my visits to terminally ill patients in the hospital where it seems safer to find fault with everything than it would be if the patient were in his or her own home, with people who would not consciously try to hurt.

As a priest, I make a good sounding board for those outbursts. I often feel it's an important part of what priests do—listen to the anger and fears of others. Family members sometimes ask me how I approach a bitter, angry person who knows his or her life is short. I tell them, "Slowly, patiently, and with great respect."

Before we get to *bargaining, depression,* and *acceptance,* we might look at the question of who should be responsible for telling the patient the bad news. In medical circles it is felt that almost always the responsibility belongs to the person who makes the diagnosis—the doctor. Dr. Kübler-Ross believes that as soon as the diagnosis is confirmed, the patient should be told that he or she is seriously ill. But then the patient should be given hope immediately and be told of all the treatment possibilities. Then the doctor should wait until the patient asks for more details.

Most doctors agree to accept the task of being the bearer of shocking news. They are generally in the best position to explain the situation quite dispassionately, and make the patient understand that everything that can be done *is* being done. But the patient must understand that this condition might possibly be terminal. I believe, as Dr. Kübler-Ross does, that no doctor should, or would, say flat out, "You're going to die." The reason, of course, is that physicians or surgeons cannot be absolutely certain that death will ensue. They are careful to leave the door slightly ajar. Of course, even this carefully worded possibility is enough to cause a patient a great deal of stress.

In line with the question, "Who tells the patient?" I am often bothered by otherwise kind, caring people who feel a great compulsion to tell others about impending doom, whether or not it's an established fact. The possibility that a friend or loved one is terminally ill often triggers rumor. And rumor becomes gossip, and gossip spreads like a brush fire and, of course, always gets back to the subject. Can you imagine anything worse than being ill and discovering that family members, friends, acquaintances, and people you don't even know very well have "heard" you are going to die?

Let's assume that someone "knows" the patient has a condition that is terminal and "feels" the doctor should have informed that patient but has not. Does anyone besides the doctor have the responsibility to tell the patient? If so, who? Can he or she do it even without the doctor's permission?

There is a rule of compassion here and it is this: No. You cannot tell a patient that his or her illness is terminal without the doctor's permission. Unless a physician delegates a minister, nurse, or social worker to do this job, it is inappropriate to do so unless one is a very close relative. For some people who thrive on gossip, the temptation is great, but the result can be emotionally devastating.

I often think of a sister of the Church, a thirty-eight-year-old nun whose lively expressions on a peaches-and-cream face made her look more like twenty-eight, who lived with a group of other sisters, a religious woman who was doing great things with children. They thought she was—in today's vernacular—pretty hip. After a short illness, Sister checked with her doctor and discovered she had ovarian cancer. As soon as she heard the cancer word, she immediately thought of her own death. Although the doctor explained to her that things have changed in the last decade, that people are living longer, that there is a lot of hope, and that cancer no longer means certain death, Sister heard only the word *cancer*. She left the office, got into the car, and just sat behind the wheel, tears streaming down her face. It took her nearly a half hour to drive away. She drove past the schoolyard, very slowly, then stopped to watch the children play. She realized that things would never again be the same for her. In her mind, a time limit had been imposed. In the weeks after, she moved into a "safer" place, a nursing home where she could find spirituality to prepare for the inevitable.

I share this story to demonstrate that death is not one-dimensional. Each individual dies similarly to the way he or she lived. There is personality involved.

I can relate to that feeling, remembering when my father was diagnosed as having colon cancer. I was with him at the far end of Long Island, in Montauk where he had a successful summer business, watching him as he looked across his property, which ran right to the shore of the Atlantic Ocean. I was at his side, but I could see his eyes and knew what was running through his mind. *Will I ever come back here? Who will take care of my wife? Who will take care of me when I can no longer take care of myself? What will the kids do with what I've built here?* I could tell he was shocked and angry. My father never shows anger physically, never throws things about the room—but I could sense the hurt.

I'm happy to say my father was operated on successfully. He still lives in Montauk, is active, and is preparing for the next stage of life: retirement with my mom.

Priests are merely people who see, feel, and experience the same mystery of death that everyone else does. Only we see a great deal more of it. Death is with us almost daily in one form or another.

I can't tell you how many hospital rooms I've been in where people are dying. After all these visits, I have discovered that while no two patients face possible terminal illness the same way, there are certain common patterns.

Often when I walk into a room, I find an angry patient. He or she will tell me the doctors are not doing anything, the nurses are not doing anything. The hospital couldn't care less about their plight. At such times there is a great temptation for the visitor to try to answer all the patient's complaints. For myself, I am happy to listen while the patient blows off steam. Then I ask simply, "Is there anything I can do?"

If there seems to be some validity to the complaints you hear, it's wise not to start a campaign against the hospital staff. I have found that talking quietly to the head nurse might help. I might say, "Can I talk with you for a moment? My friend is a little upset. I know this is a difficult time for him, and he wonders if you might help him by attending to this or that..." This approach shows respect for the profession of the nurse, and it invites the healthcare professional to be on your team. You might ask the professional if there's anything you can do, or anything that you should be aware of. Your quiet concern could make things better all around.

A priest often hears a patient *bargaining*. While some people who realize that time is short might issue silent vows, it is the priest, minister, or rabbi who is most likely to hear them articulated. You hear, "Wait a minute! There's something that I didn't do that I should have done. There's something I could have done better. I want to make amends for hurting someone I didn't know I was hurting. I want people to remember me in a different light. I want to say things I've never said before. I want to say what's in my heart. I want to talk with a man of God. Maybe God will grant me more if He knows what I want to do, if He knows how badly I want to reform."

When my aunt was diagnosed with cancer, she made her "bargain with God" early on. Aunt Gerry said, "I have six kids. All but one is grown up, but the youngest is only twelve." She prayed that she would be given "two more years, just two." Her prayer was answered and she got those two years, and she seemed immensely relieved and maintained an unusually good frame of mind. But a bargain is never a guarantee. A bargain generally begins as a form of panic, and there is nothing wrong with that—it may even have a little therapeutic value. Actually, I feel that most "bargains with God" are made by people who know full well that God doesn't run a wish-fulfillment service. However, some think it's worth a try—and who am I to say it isn't?

The next phase some patients enter is the one that bothers me most: *depression.* Depression is a very vexing problem and must be handled with extreme care. Depression hurts not only the patients, but those around them, especially those who love and care about them.

When the prognosis indicates no hope, when a patient is convinced that the days are numbered, that death is imminent, life's priorities change dramatically. "Things" lose all importance. Things will be left behind. Memories will count. Unfilled duties will float to the top of the list. The care of one's beloved after death will be a paramount concern.

I received a telephone call from a woman I'd

known for some years asking me to talk with a friend of hers who was dying of cancer but who was still lucid and ambulatory. When I contacted the woman, she insisted on coming to me since my visiting her house might raise undue concern among her children. Also she wanted to talk in a place where she would not be overheard or, worse, misunderstood.

She turned out to be an extremely attractive woman whose demeanor belied the fact that she was ill. Except for the lines around her eyes and mouth, you wouldn't guess she was suffering both confusion and depression.

"I'm forty-three years old," she said, "and I have cancer. What I need right now is somebody to talk to. I know I'm dying, and I want to discuss a few things as objectively as possible without having to dance around the subject." Such candor was refreshing. "I am certain my husband and children love me very much, and they will never know how much I really love them. The most difficult thing I'm facing right now, outside of the pain and the embarrassment of having them do things for me, is— well, communicating. When I start to discuss my love for my children, the task becomes unbearable. When the tears start, they somehow get the wrong message. I cry and then they cry, and what I want to say doesn't get said."

We chatted about other things for a while and then returned to the specifics of her problem. "Your family obviously loves you, and this is a great jolt for them as well as for you. I would guess that you can talk to me more easily than you can talk to them. That's why we are together now. I have an idea that might help move you beyond this emotional impasse. I would like you to do something special."

"Special? What?"

"I'd like you to write a few notes during your rest time. A note to your husband, explaining just how you feel about him. Recall in writing the first time you met and what there was about him that caused you to fall in love with him. Remind him of exciting and pleasure-filled moments when you were together.

"Then I want you to write a similar note to each of your children. Remind them of their tender years, of the fun you had with them on vacation, the school events you saw them in, and how much you love and admire them.

"These don't have to be long notes, and they don't have to be sad notes. They should be little letters they'll want to read, put away, and keep. Each of your children is different in some special way, and a note of affirmation of that particular individual would be very personal and meaningful to that specific child. And the same with your husband."

She said she would try it and get back to me. She smiled when she left, and I could tell she was obviously thinking it over.

In the days that followed I spoke with each of the children and told them that they would each receive a note from their mother. They should thank her and talk about what she had to say. The notes were written and handed out one by one, and each child, separately, discussed the contents with the mother.

"It was a fine idea," she said later. "It opened up some doors for me, and you were right. Each of my kids *is* different, so some of the notes were funny and some were quite serious. There was something else I've been thinking about since I wrote the notes. I thought I might buy each child a gold ring to have after I'm gone."

"Why not buy the rings now and hand them out one by one?" I asked. "You see, when your will is read, the rings will only be part of a larger formality. You might think about giving them the opportunity now to say 'Thanks, Mom' and show their true devotion. I think it would make them feel good, and you will have made another connection."

At the wake, I was surrounded by her youngsters, all wearing their rings. All with a beautiful memory of the last days with their mother.

This approach seemed to work in this particular case. It isn't my "stock answer" to a communications problem. I have learned over the years that there is no "best" way. There are many ways to help prepare another human for the inevitable.

I had just been ordained and was very new at this business of bereavement and was actually quite honored when I got a call from a woman we'll call Sandra, a very active member of the parish where I was stationed at the time. I had met her husband only once at a parish spring dance. The telephone message was: "Can I see you?"

I returned her call and invited her to meet with me.

"I'll have to come alone."

"No problem," I said.

She was the picture of anguish when she arrived and had difficulty with even the pleasantries of the weather and how the kids were doing in school. She took a deep breath and said, "It's about Joe."

Joe, her husband, was a no-nonsense detective on the New York City police force and a man with whom you'd think twice about doing battle.

"What about Joe?"

"He's dying, and I would like it very much if you would talk with him. Since the diagnosis, I don't know what to do with him. I just look at him and want to burst out crying. He's still a very young man, and so tough. I didn't think anything could bring him down."

"I'll be glad to talk with him," I said.

"Fine," she hesitated, "but he's not very religious. And he's tough and he doesn't want any big sympathy deal. I mean, if he could just sort of talk this thing out with somebody who isn't going to break down and fall all over him."

"I know what you mean. See if you can get him

to stop by one of these evenings. I think it would be best if we talked awhile away from the home."

About a week later Joe showed up at the rectory looking most uneasy. He sat across the desk from me, his ample, muscular body filling the chair, his broad shoulders back, his blazer barely hiding the police revolver he was required to carry at all times. He certainly didn't look sick. Upset, perhaps, but sick, no. There were no pleasantries, no chit-chat— maybe he wasn't used to that in his work. He opened up full volume.

"I'm not a fish," he said. "I'm a whale. I'm thirty-seven years old. I'm a cop. I bench-press three hundred fifty pounds." There was a long pause. "I have a wife and three kids, and I have less than a year to live." A flat-out statement. A confession. "Can you help me?"

You must remember, I was quite new at this. Here was a challenge from a man I barely knew, a parishioner but not a churchgoer, with an intimidating personality asking a young priest for help. At that moment, neither of us had any idea what kind of help he needed. Here was a man, I thought, who was only twelve years my senior looking down the road a year from now and was in great denial, but all the same frightened. To Joe, impending death was an embarrassment, an affront to the body he had built up.

I was experienced enough to know that both Joe and his wife were very uncomfortable on my turf, so I suggested he give me a day or two to think over his situation, and perhaps I could make a call at their home at some convenient time.

"Anytime after noon during the week would be okay," he said. "I work nights, and the kids will be in school."

"I could do that."

"See," Joe said, "I really would appreciate it if nobody knew I came over here to see you, and maybe if you came to see me you could wear regular clothes. Can you do that?"

"Certainly," I said. "The collar is my uniform in church, but I can wear something else…."

"It isn't that I'd be embarrassed or anything," he said. "It's just that it'd be better for the kids and my friends if nobody knew…"

"…that I was a priest. That's all right with me." *For now*, I thought.

Sandra invited me to lunch—Joe's breakfast—and over coffee Joe told me a little bit about his illness. He said he was diagnosed after a blood work-up and some x-rays, but he didn't yet have the symptoms that would indicate a terminal condition. Oh, he got a little more tired than usual after an eight-hour night shift, and he had a few aches and pains—stiffness in the legs—but didn't everybody go through that? "Let me show you the kind of shape I'm in," he said. Joe took me downstairs where he had created quite a well-equipped workout room. He showed me how he lifted weights, particularly a hundred-pound metal piece that he maneuvered very handily.

"Here, you try it, Father."

I was in pretty good shape myself, but it was obvious that he was much stronger sick than I was well. I took a rain check.

As the afternoon wore on, we traded stories about his police work and about my parish duties. After a bit, I realized that here was this very macho guy befriending me, and I had become probably one of the very first persons he ever trusted enough to share his vulnerability.

Joe told me that day there was no question that he would beat "this rap." He would work out more, take it a little easier on the job, maybe even ask for a transfer to day duty, although he really liked the action on the night detail.

But as time crept along, he realized that the doctors were quite on target and he asked for a leave of absence from his detail. He began a series of treatments that caused him to become unsettled and angry. He hated the drugs. They made him sick. Every visit to his doctor's office was painful in more ways than one. He couldn't understand how his great body had betrayed him. He had spent so much time perfecting it. He drew more and more inward. He saw few friends, even though several fellow officers wanted to visit him, take him to a ball game, dinner, or a show.

Finally, his oldest son, Josh, came to visit me.

He said, "My father is dying and he won't talk to us about it."

A few days later, I paid Joe a visit. "Your son came to see me. He wonders why you won't talk to him about your condition and what the future might hold."

"I can't," Joe said. "My kids have never seen me weak. They've never seen me sick. If they know I'm going to die, then they'd know. *You* talk to them. *You're* the expert in this stuff."

I said, "Joe, you're asking me to take over your responsibility. A good cop won't do that."

Joe began to cough, trying to rid his lungs of phlegm. In the struggle, tears rolled down his cheeks. He threw off the covers. "Look at me! A lousy hundred thirty pounds!" I pulled the covers back around him. His wife was standing in the doorway of the bedroom. I asked her to come in. "I'm going outside to get the oils. I'm going to anoint you, Joe. Talk to Sandra."

I purposely stayed outside a rather long time, more than the ten minutes I needed. When I returned, I saw the two of them holding each other and crying. It was the first time he had talked to his wife about dying—he had held it in that long. "Why don't I run downstairs to get the boys, Joe? They're trying to watch television, but I don't think they're seeing it."

"Okay, Father," Joe said.

After an hour or so, I anointed Joe and heard his confession and the two of us talked again. As I started to leave, he said, "No, you stay awhile." I sat with Joe another half hour or so, both of us absolutely silent. Finally, Joe looked up and said, "You can leave now."

It had been a highly emotional night for Sandra and the three boys, but she managed a smile through the tears as I left.

Joe died that night.

I relate these stories to encourage anyone in similar situations to share thoughts, perceptions, and knowledge with the living and to make at least some sort of plans for that unavoidable moment of separation.

And so we come to the last story: *acceptance.*

When someone is dying, and you know it and he or she knows it, there must still be a communication. As a priest, the only gift I can give is my ability to help make the patient as comfortable as possible emotionally and spiritually. I can ask a patient, "Would you like to talk about your death?" or "Is there something you want to do?"

Remember my Aunt Gerry who made a "bargain" with God, asking for two more years to get her children started on the right path. After that two-year "reprieve," I received a call from my dad saying, "Aunt Gerry is very ill."

I called my uncle—her husband—and asked, "Can I go to see her?"

"She'd like that," he said.

On my way to the hospital, the image of Aunt

Gerry some years ago formed crystal clear in my head. A mother of six, she knew death firsthand. One of her children died shortly after birth. She had been a wonderful mother, a real caretaker of the family. Her faith in God was absolutely unshakable.

I had no idea what we would talk about when I arrived at the hospital in Bay Shore, Long Island, but when I walked into her room, I felt not at all anxious and was, in fact, very calm. I saw Aunt Gerry raised only slightly in the bed, her face drawn but the remnants of a strong person still showing through.

We smiled at each other, and she motioned for me to sit beside her bed.

"How do you feel?" I asked.

"I'm dying, Tom."

"I know." There was a pause, then I said, "How do you feel about that?"

Her response surprised me somewhat. "I'm looking forward to it. Ever since I was a little girl, I always had a deep love for the Blessed Mother, and I always wanted to meet Her. When I got sick two years ago, I talked with the Blessed Mother. I said, 'You're a mother. I'm a mother. I need two more years to prepare my child—my youngest. Just give me two more years.'"

Another pause. I said, "Do you have any regrets, Aunt Gerry?"

"Yes. Not for any pain I've been through. That's not important. My only regret is when I look into the eyes of the people who love me, knowing the pain they have, knowing what they are going through, and knowing I can't take that pain away for them. Tom," she said, "I've been reading about some of the things you're doing in the media. Keep it up. It shows your faith, and we need more faith, we need more family today. Oh, how the world needs faith!"

At that moment my Uncle Walter entered the room and leaned over to kiss his wife. "How are you doing today, Gerry?"

"I'm fine. How are things on Wall Street, Walter? Did we make a bundle for anybody today?"

"Not today. Maybe tomorrow."

Then she asked him, "What did the doctor tell you about those x-rays, Walter? How are we doing with the pneumonia and the lungs? If we could only get that pneumonia, Walter, then we'd have it," she said.

"Right, Babe."

A short while later when Uncle Walter and I left the room, I put my arm around his shoulder and asked, "Why don't you talk to Aunt Gerry about her death?"

He stopped, stunned. "She *knows?*"

"Of course she knows," I said. "We had been talking about it when you came in."

Uncle Walter turned, left me, and walked back into Gerry's room.

The next day he told me they spent over an hour talking about how they met, the kids, their hopes when they were newlyweds—and about her funeral. She was to live only a few more days. Uncle Walter said he was forever grateful for my being so "thoughtfully direct."

Uncle Walter was suddenly free—this is what happens when you can deal with and get over the fact that someone is ready to die. It frees you—and you can "allow" the person to die.

Let go. Let God.

4

THE GUILT SYNDROME

It is my practice at the close of the Mass to go to the back of church so I might get better acquainted with my people, and my parishioners might get to know me better. Of course, in a parish the size of the one I serve, it is difficult to know everybody personally. I like having the people who have seen me celebrate their Mass shake my hand and think of me as something of an anchor.

In the course of this exercise one Sunday an eighty-three-year-old man, who regularly attended this particular Mass, stopped to chat. His thinning white hair, his lined face, and his tenuous smile reminded me of a Norman Rockwell painting. His pale blue eyes met mine and in a soft but anxious tone he startled me, saying, "Father, if my wife dies, could you come and give her the last rites?" It's actually called Anointing of the Sick, but I knew what he meant, and I said, "Certainly." Then he was lost among the departing assemblage.

I had agreed to visit the man's wife, but I didn't expect the call to come so soon. Only a few weeks later, at seven in the morning, he called to say, "Father, I think my wife is dead. Could you come to the house?"

There are certain calls the rectory receives that have priority. This is one of them. When a friend calls with this kind of plea, you go immediately.

The man was waiting at the front door when I arrived and ushered me into the living room. With a whisper, he showed me where the bedroom was. He preferred to stay in the living room, he said, but urged me to look at his wife where she lay.

It appeared to me that his wife had been dead for a couple of hours. I anointed her and then walked to the living room to talk with him.

"Father, did my wife die?"

When I looked at him, it was apparent that he was hoping she hadn't.

"Yes. I believe your wife has died," I replied in the softest voice I could find. Never had a room been so still.

He looked through the front window and saw my car. It was new. "Pretty sharp car you've got there, Father. Pretty spiffy. Looks brand new."

"It is," I said. "Even a priest needs a good car these days."

There was a pause. "Do I hear you on the radio sometimes?"

"You might."

"Is that you with that rock-and-roll program?"

"Yes. It's one way of reaching the kids."

"Father. Did my wife die?"

Then I realized what was happening. We were building a sudden relationship. This man had lived with the woman I just anointed for sixty years. She was his everything. Even through the painful years of her cancer, he devoted his entire life to her every day. She was the center of his life. If he really understood all the implications of her death immediately, he would emotionally short-circuit. He was in shock, an emotional buffer that keeps us sane when the raw truth is too much for us.

From then on, he would need someone to be there for him. He would need a family member, a friend, someone who would visit him so he could talk about his wife, tell stories about their life together, how much he loved her, the places they'd been, and the things they saw together. Even after the wake and funeral, I visited him regularly myself, but it was obvious that he needed someone to see and talk to and touch. His wife's death put him in a traumatic state somewhat like a twilight zone, which is probably why he couldn't go into the bedroom on the day she died until after I arrived. He simply couldn't bear to see her go, even though the signs were clear. He needed a friend—someone who had traveled this road before.

Another example of the need for emotional sustenance has quite the reverse story. A woman called to tell me that her father died, and she wanted to know what she had to do next. My answer was simple and obvious. "Call an undertaker." She didn't know of one. I recommended a mortician in her village whom I knew would render the proper service at a reasonable price. She asked me to call, which I was happy to do because it would give me a chance to tell the people at the mortuary that this family needed help.

I knew their background, although I had only met the father a few times. He was the classic bad guy patriarch: an alcoholic, a gambler, and a violent person. Both the daughter who called me and her mother, the man's wife, had suffered several beatings and innumerable emotional attacks by this difficult and destructive person. All her life, the daughter had been terrified of this man—even after she married and left home. She worried constantly about the welfare of her mother.

I had counseled the daughter on a half dozen occasions, generally after an eruption of violence in the home caused by the man's drinking and tantrums. There was no chance that he would receive counseling. He was not a member of the Church, and was prone to outbursts whenever the Church was even mentioned. I surmised that the Church represented a threat of some kind to him. He was clearly in need of psychological help.

Despite the turmoil he caused, and actual physical and emotional damage he wrought during the past forty-or-so years, the police were never called, an order of protection was never sought. In fact, the daughter and her mother invented any number of excuses to hide his erratic behavior. It became natural for them to avoid scandal.

When the man died after mistreating his body over the years, both the mother and the daughter felt a great, tearful relief. They were happy that he was gone.

Yet they would discover that even though a person has been very difficult and destructive, there still remains a connection. The emotional mix here is relief, guilt, and anger. In this instance, the daughter and the mother were so angry, all they could think to do was to have the man cremated.

They asked me, "Does the Church allow cremation?" Years ago it did not, I explained, but then the bishops in England realized that burial spaces were becoming scarce, so some sanctions were amended. A body can now be cremated if the individual believes there is an afterlife. The man's daughter and wife said they believed he did, as non-religious as he professed to be. I had to accept that.

Then I asked them, "Do you want to have a wake?"

"No."

"Do you want to have a Mass?"

"No."

"Suppose I say a memorial Mass for your dad?"

They said they would like that and asked me if I would handle it for them. All they wanted to do was cremate the man.

I knew that in a couple of months I would have to visit these two women again. It would be my opportunity to allay some of the guilt they would be feeling by then. I could go there and, in effect, give them permission to be angry, to be disappointed, to feel relief, but at the same time not to give up on the man. That's an interesting part of our faith. No matter how bad people are, we leave it to God to judge them and to bring about spiritual transformation. In that way, the mother and the daughter can let go, as if to say, "He was thoughtless and mean, and he hurt us a lot, but we hope that in the next world with God he can see the error of his ways."

Guilt is a strange emotion. In fact, the guilt reaction is often set in one's mind at a very early age, when children first ask the question, "Why?"

Many people feel a twinge of guilt when they are questioned about something about which they know virtually nothing. Often the very presence of a police officer can bring on guilt pangs even though you haven't done anything, aren't planning to do anything, and in fact would never entertain a criminal thought. And so it is after the death of a loved one.

Psychologists generally put guilt into two categories: real guilt—the kind of guilt one feels when he or she has actually caused someone harm or done someone a disservice—and manic, or neurotic, guilt. This is the kind of guilt that is not only unreasonable but totally out of proportion to real involvement.

In the two extremely different stories I've related here, there are obvious manifestations of guilt. In the case of the elderly man, his guilt lay in the worry that he had not taken good enough care of his wife, that he was afraid to be at her side after he believed she had gone. He felt guilty about his uneasiness in being able to handle the situation without help, and he felt he had somehow cheated his wife in not being the first one to go, as unreasonable as the latter might seem. There is almost always a tinge of guilt where there is grief. One may ask, "Is there anything at all I could have done to help prevent this loss? Is there anything I could have done to make the passing easier? What did this loved one think of me while still alive?"

And here is an emotional trap that many of us fall into. It is a question that belies an individual's security: "What will people think of *me*?" This, of course, following the death of a family member or friend, is the last thing you should consider. What anybody thinks about you is of no consequence. For the most part, mourners will be oblivious to all but their sincere sympathy during your bereavement.

In the case of the mother and the daughter, they had every right to be angry and relieved, yet questions will remain with them for years. Could either of them understand that they were *not* the root cause of this man's behavior, that the only resolution would have been for him to recognize his own problems and get help from a counselor? These women were, as a jury might declare, "Not guilty."

There is a distinct danger in manic—or neurotic—guilt. It can actually make you sick. When you suddenly have to face the death of a loved one, the tendency is to go back over your life looking for and worrying about things—little and large—that you may have done to hurt the deceased. An argument, an unkind word, a burst of temper, or neglect. Guilt may stem from an aversion to being with or even near a person who is dying.

A good example of neurotic grief might be a daughter who stayed at the bedside of her ailing father until the strain was beginning to endanger her own health. She finally asked another member of the family to take her place for a night or two. During that time, her father died, and for years the daughter could never forgive herself for not being at her father's side, holding his hand, when he passed away. That is unnecessary manic guilt, the kind that will never let you find true peace. It will hurt more than help. No forgiveness is necessary.

If you find yourself reviewing what is no longer possible to amend, understand that it's not only normal, but healthy—and move *beyond* guilt. Wipe the slate clean. There is nothing you can do now. Only the body remains. The soul is with God and whatever lapses you may be able to count—real or otherwise—he or she is in the hands of God, and God will take it from there.

In the Catholic Church we have confession in which even the mildest of sinners might feel a remarkable sense of relief by visiting the confessional before receiving Holy Communion. Catholics are taught about the divine gift of forgiveness, and we hope they never fear the admission of real guilt followed by genuine repentance.

5

A CHILD DIES

The pairing of the words *innocence* and *death* seems to create a form of grief for which there *are* no words—as with the death of a child. This sadness is not confined to parents. Except for the most uncaring, thoughtless, and evil, losing a child is an extremely painful experience. We care about our own, love them, adore them, and would do anything for them.

Unfortunately—tragically—not all children are looked on as God's miracles. As you read this, fifteen million children are starving to death, and not all of them in faraway countries where we can put them out of our minds. Nurses from the United Nations Health Food Program see their daily task as setting up death sites for the children of Somalia, where little ones who have starved to death are brought by wheelbarrow to be lined up for burial. In each of these centers, nurses watch a dozen or so children die every day.

We have seen graphic photographs showing the horrors of Sarajevo and Bosnia, pictures of children whose limbs have been shot off by young, eager enemy soldiers who have been given guns and consider human targets fair game, no matter the age.

Television shows us a child's casket, painted in white lacquer, placed on the grass at the edge of the Roman Catholic cemetery in Sarajevo, where two women in black come to claim it. They plead with the television reporter to beckon a photographer with a still camera to take a photo.

"Please take a picture," the younger woman, the mother, says. "I have none." She opens the lid, revealing a vast space for her tiny son. The little boy was the youngest of ten victims buried that day—all of them children. Thousands of children brave sniper and shellfire as they rush to attend the first day of school in the outskirts of the town.

In all the cities in South America, skinny, underfed "street kids" follow picnickers and wait for them to finish eating, hoping they will leave a cookie, half a sandwich, an apple core. The mortality rate is staggering.

The United States, our own country, the nation we consider "most civilized," is also setting a bad example. In our large metropolitan centers, not just New York, more children than we want to count are dying from gunshot wounds, caught in the crossfire of drug dealers. Even bed isn't safe for them in their ghettos. Any American relief organization can tell you how many thousands of our children are undernourished and will probably starve to death this year, how many need serious medical attention they are not getting, and how many are actually killed by child abuse.

Fact: One million children disappear every year in the United States, and of these one million, *a hundred thousand* end up somewhere in a morgue without leaving any clue as to what they experienced between the moment they left their homes and the time they met their death somewhere away from home.

These observations are not meant to soften the blow of the loss of a child, but to point out that since the beginning of so-called civilization, children have been victimized, exploited, hurt, and destroyed.

There was a time in America when families lived in the same communities for generations, when everyone knew *the* pastor, *the* doctor, *the* grocer, and knew their neighbors by their first names, when children had a sense of belonging, when the whole community awaited the birth of a newcomer. Today we don't know much about our neighbors, let alone who owns the supermarket or the first names of the specialists our doctors send us to. Today many couples decide it's better to have a career and security first and perhaps a child later. It's better, they feel, to pay for a house or apartment before being "tied down."

This makes for a remarkable revelation later on. When their baby does come along, the worldly-wise, educated parents understand—more than they ever would have in their younger years—the impact of the miracle that has been bestowed upon them. The baby! Their pledge for the future! The part of their very bodies and souls that will live on.

But then, too, in a family where children begin arriving early, there is also awe in the first signs of life, in the baby's first cry, the little fingers and toes, the very breath of the tiny being. As time goes by in this family, older brothers and sisters will look in wonder at the tiny creature who has become their brother or sister.

No matter the social situation, it is rare that a mother would reject her own child, that a father would ignore his child's wants and needs. So despite what is happening to children—the world's most precious asset—the American parent and kin find the death of a child an especially sad and trying event.

Advising and counseling the bereaved when a child dies is a very complicated matter for pastoral caregivers because there are so many ramifications that lead to the same sad ending. A mother might have her child taken away at birth, and never be allowed to touch or hold the child. The baby may be stillborn. The doctors may recognize a life-threatening physical condition in the child that would call for years of special care before the child dies. The severe trauma in the disappointment at the birth creates a completely new set of conditions to be considered. There is no one way to help soften the impact on the parents of a dead or dying baby.

It is even more stressful when the child begins to grow up and develops a personality, as he or she becomes intellectually bonded with the mother and father.

Then, too, we have a very sensitive situation between the mother and father. For example, the doctor may instruct the father not to upset his wife in any way. The mother then wonders why her husband doesn't show more emotion. Most psychologists I've encountered suggest that the parents do what feels right inside—that intuitive honesty increases the chances of solving conflicts.

Perhaps even more heartbreaking to loving parents is the sudden death of a child. I recall a young couple I knew very well—I married them—who were justifiably proud of their little boy, Brandon. Both Jim and Sara agreed that God had answered their prayers. At three, Brandon was developing into a healthy, sturdy young man with a sense of humor that matched his father's. Jim could hardly wait until Brandon was old enough to take fishing. Jim's boat was his fourth love, and he fantasized the day when Brandon would be at the wheel. The boat was moored in a slip adjoining their property on Long Island—a familiar sight in this part of the country.

One day—somehow—Brandon decided to explore the wonders of his backyard and toddled toward the slip where the boat was tied. Sara felt, as mothers do, a sudden silence in the house. Then, a slight panic, and called Brandon's name. No answer. She looked in his room, in their own room, in the closets, and even in the basement. She called again and again and again. *Could he have unlocked the screen door and gone outside?* Sara flew out the back door screaming Brandon's name. This alarmed and alerted her friend next door. The two women, in a concert of fear, scoured the area. Sara thought the unthinkable. The boat!

When she and her friend pushed the boat away from the slip, she saw a tiny form floating next to the pier. The village rescue team arrived in what seemed seconds, but it was too late. The shock almost killed Sara.

Who would call Jim in Manhattan? What would she do next? A second was an hour.

It was a rather long drive for me, and when I arrived I found two people so distraught that it seemed the grief would completely break both of them. This was not a time for rationale, and certainly not a time for "ifs"—or blame. As in many cases before, the best thing I could do was to "be there" for them. On the horizon I could see clouds of guilt that would develop into storms of rage. Sara would never forgive herself. Jim would secretly hold Sara responsible for some time before he would be able to

see that it could have been his own back that was
turned for that instant.

An unthinking neighbor, of course, uttered the
worst possible words of compassion. "Well, you two
are young yet. You can always look forward to
another baby." If any suggestion could dampen their
lives at that point, that was it.

The parents, brothers, sisters, relatives, and
friends who surrounded Sara and Jim at this low
point in their lives were extremely helpful in keeping
the two of them—especially Sara—on an even keel.
It was a time when these two young people needed
all the faith they could muster, and I was extremely
gratified that their faith was there. It was a true crisis
in their marriage and would have a profound effect
on how they felt about each other for the rest of their
lives. Nothing shakes the soul like the death of a
child.

Sara and Jim were able to find a time and place
where they could finally open up and share their
feelings, where they could scream without frightening each other, where they could attack the matter
of blame, where they could weep for "what might
have been," and where they could remember Brandon
for the short time they had him. Although they
never discussed the prospect of having more children,
within five years they had two more, a boy and a girl.
The reaffirmation of their love for each other was
reflected in the birth of both those babies.

Brandon was never forgotten, and often cried

over, but this family found a way to continue—and grow. Their faith saw them through, for after a while, when the support of parents, relatives, and friends faded away, not in any uncaring sense, their lives went on. It was something only Sara and Jim could do with the help of faith.

Another painful kind of loss is sudden infant death syndrome—SIDS. I have in my journals a letter from a wonderful woman named Dorothy, a friend of mine whose baby, Keith, died of this tragic syndrome about ten years ago. Dorothy was so articulate and direct in her reaction that I'd like to share her thoughts with you. She wrote, in part:

"Keith was a beautiful, healthy little boy, born at a particularly difficult time for my family as my father had died of cancer only two weeks before. He was a joy, and it helped knowing that my father would have been happy and as pleased as the rest of us. We were totally unprepared when six weeks later this healthy little baby would die during his sleep, a victim of sudden infant death syndrome.

"It is difficult to find the words to express the intense pain and emotional turmoil that a parent feels when a child dies. Certainly shock, devastation, loneliness, and denial are all part of trying to cope, but there is also an enormous sense of responsibility for the child's life.

"He was so little and depended on us for everything. How could I have failed him? And how would I live without him? Everywhere I looked there were reminders. All of the things in his room, the lost pacifier under the couch, the box of diapers in the closet, his brother's questions about where he was, and our difficulty in finding answers to the endless questions.

"Maybe if I had checked him sooner; if I hadn't taken him out the day before; if I had shown my love more often. Why did he have to die?

"From what we read, we were to learn that eight thousand babies die every year from SIDS—all just like Keith, apparently normal, healthy babies who die very quickly in their sleep. We learned that there was no way to predict or prevent Keith's death, and most importantly, it wasn't our fault. An autopsy was performed, but revealed nothing significant enough to have caused his death; in fact, it revealed nothing at all. The diagnosis of sudden infant death syndrome is one of exclusion. When a baby dies suddenly and unexpectedly, with no history of prior illness, and the autopsy finds nothing, it is listed as SIDS.

"All the information we read was comforting, but couldn't bring back our son. We had no chance to offer prayers or promises. He was gone and no one could change that. We found comfort and support from a number of people who loved and cared about us, but most unexpectedly from a group of people we didn't know—other parents who had also lost a child to SIDS.

"Soon after Keith's death, our pediatrician put

us in touch with a volunteer organization known as the Sudden Infant Death Syndrome Alliance. This organization consisted primarily of other parents who had lost a child to SIDS. We were supplied with information which we found helpful, but these people also gave us a part of themselves which was far more valuable. This group arranged for two members of their organization to visit with us at home. A nurse and another parent, who had also lost a child, came to our house. I was amazed that this parent, who spoke to us during that first visit, appeared to be so 'normal.' How could that possibly be? She, too, had lost a child. Was she showing me that it was possible to survive? It was then that I discovered the first glimmer of hope that maybe Keith's death wouldn't be so painful and so unbelievably hard to live with. I decided to become involved with this group. There had to be an answer as to why Keith died, and I wanted to join in the fight against SIDS.

"The goals of the SIDS Alliance are to assist parents who have lost a child, educate the community about SIDS, and stimulate research so that someday an answer might be found. In the beginning, our involvement 'to help others' was really more a need to help ourselves. Both my husband and I started attending general meetings. We became involved in fund raising and, finally, about a year later, we began talking with parents who had recently lost a child. I wanted to be there for someone else as others had been there for me.

"Two years after Keith's death, we had another baby—a beautiful little girl. Because of my involvement with the SIDS Alliance, I was aware of the research going on at that time into the possible causes of SIDS. One area of particular interest had to do with *apnea*—a cessation of breathing during sleep. There was a suggestion that this might possibly be a contributing factor to sudden infant death syndrome. Jamie, our new daughter, was evaluated by a physician, and found to have frequent periods of apnea, which required her to be on a monitor at home for the first year of her life. So many times during that first year I thought that we may have to face the loss of another child. I was very frightened for her—and for all of us—wondering if we could survive such a loss again.

"Jamie outgrew her apnea by the time she was a year old. Most children do. But the result of that experience was a confirmation of our commitment to continue our efforts to find a cure for this frightening disease, and to work with other parents until the answer can be found."

You can see why I kept and treasured Dorothy's letter.

Dorothy kept up her great works with the SIDS Alliance, serving several years as a parent contact, editor of the local newsletter, and vice president for special projects. By the time Dorothy became president of the regional foundation, her own need for the support of others had ebbed, but she couldn't ignore the parents who still needed her support. She found the rewards of helping others enormous. Some people couldn't understand how Dorothy and her husband could remain involved for so long a period, but Dorothy says today that it meant more than she could ever explain.

In her research and alignment with the Alliance, Dorothy found that in some cases of SIDS, parents were mistreated, ignored, or cut off following their child's death. "As in our situation," she says, "a number of babies who die of SIDS die during the night. It may be several hours before the parents awaken to find the baby lifeless."

Post mortem changes, which occur after death, will cause a pooling of the blood and at times distortion of the baby's face. A police officer arriving on the scene who is unfamiliar with SIDS may suspect that these are signs of abuse, as even some medical professionals might. Because SIDS is the leading cause of death in children during the first year of life, the education of the professional and lay community is an area of priority for the SIDS Alliance, as well as involved parents.

Parents such as Dorothy and her husband fought for and won, finally, an appropriation of federal funds to start programs in local communities so that

- An autopsy will be performed on all of these babies to determine the cause of death;

- The parents will be notified of the autopsy results within twenty-four hours, where previously some parents had to wait for months to find out the cause of death of their child;
- The wording "sudden infant death syndrome" will be used instead of "unknown" or "undetermined" as had generally been the case; and
- Education is made available to the community, especially the police, medical examiners, physicians, nurses, emergency medical technicians, funeral directors, the clergy, and all members of the general community, so that all parents involved in such a tragedy will be treated with sensitivity and compassion.

Over the last decade federal funding has increased dramatically and the SIDS Alliance can take credit for making great inroads in making all of us aware of the very existence of this disease.*

While Dorothy's work with the SIDS Alliance continues, she has gone on to make her new life count even more. She returned to school full time to complete a master's degree in Social Welfare.

Talking about her grief, Dorothy says, "Another parent asked me how long it took to 'get over' Keith's death. I tried, but couldn't affix a time. But if 'getting over' meant that it was no longer painful, that I wasn't depressed, and that I no longer loved him or missed him, then I would never be over it."

Dorothy's story is an excellent example of one

way to face a heartbreaking crisis. But the loss of a child comes in so many scenarios, that it's impossible to formulate a single pat answer on how to help alleviate the stress of bereavement.

I have one memory that will never leave me. The incident happened in the obstetrics section of Good Samaritan Hospital in West Islip, New York. I had been visiting a new mother who had recently moved from our parish, but who wanted me to see and bless the new baby girl. We had a very pleasant visit, and I had an opportunity to meet her husband and his parents. A joyful time. A beautiful baby. As is my habit, I checked with the head nurse on the floor before going into the new mother's room, and on the way out, I thanked her. The nurse motioned for me to come to the end of the nursing station where she might talk to me in private.

"I'm worried about the teenage girl in room 32," the head nurse said.

"Why? What's the problem?" I asked.

She looked at the chart. "She's seventeen. Her baby was stillborn. Her mother brought her in and has been back only twice—at night. I didn't want to ask, but it looks as if this young girl has only a mother. No other relatives. No other visitors. And I haven't seen hide nor hair of anyone who might be the baby's father."

"And she's alone almost all the time?"

"That's right, Father. It's not that she'd do anything foolish, but the poor kid just lies there and

stares at the wall. She won't even turn on the
television set. I wonder if you'd..."

"Go in and say hello?"

"I don't know if she's Catholic."

"What difference would that make? It's no
crime to say hello. What's her name?"

"Christiana. Christiana Ekstrom."

I knocked gently on the door of room 32. No
sound. I knocked again. I heard a soft moan. I opened
the door slowly, looked quickly, then stepped in. I
saw a pale, thin, drawn, blond young woman whose
eyes were unrealistically pale.

"Christiana?" Silence. "Chris?"

She sat up slowly. She stared at me, and looked
to see if there was anyone behind me. The door
closed softly, and I looked about the room. A flower
arrangement, but no cards, no gifts, no phone—just
the usual hospital paraphernalia. That was it. The
moment was a little strained.

"How are you, Chris? I'm Father Tom. Is there
anything I can do for you or get for you?"

She trembled imperceptibly, then almost in a
rush, held out her arms to me. I walked to the bed and
embraced her. Her body was convulsed with sobs. I
could feel her tears covering her cheeks. She cried
for several minutes, and even when there didn't
seem to be any tears left, she still clung to me.

As wan as this young woman seemed to be, her
physical strength was amazing. Something told me
that she hadn't hugged or been hugged for a very

long time. I stayed with her, and we talked for about a half hour. She wasn't a font of clinical information, but we had a very pleasant chat. I knew she felt much better when she ran out of words, so I left. I had no reason to interrogate her, I had no need to know about her life unless she offered the information. I could guess what her situation was, and that was enough for the time I was with her.

I visited Christiana one more time before she left the hospital, and I never discovered any more about her than I learned the day I met her. Her mother was present the last time I saw Christiana, and she thanked me for looking in on her daughter. I saw Christiana smile that day and that, for the moment, was enough.

I tell this only to introduce this thought: Sometimes the bereaved need only a shoulder to cry on. Anything more is too much.

The loss of a child is unlike any other loss. The emotional trauma is more severe for several reasons. The child is innocent, but often experiences more than one setback if, for example, he or she is suffering from a terminal illness and must undergo a series of operations, each with a recovery period, each with its own pain. Then there are what the French call "little deaths": The loss of hair from chemotherapy, the use of crutches, then the introduction to the wheelchair, and finally the adjustable bed.

The parents suffer vicariously observing their child's inability to walk, to dance, to kick a football, to go to a prom, to gallivant with friends, to fall in love, to marry. There will be no grandchildren.

The little patient finally wants to see fewer and fewer people. The weariness begins to show, and the parents see their child fade, and, finally, silently slip away. The anguish and agony of long and expensive medical procedures are finally over, but will leave lifelong scars. The brothers and sisters who have been put into secondary positions in the family now resume their priority roles, leaving them with a certain unspoken bitterness, a sense of unfairness, and a tremendous amount of guilt.

A distraught parent may wonder, "Would sudden death be better?" Then hate herself or himself for even entertaining the thought, for sudden death can bring on a frightful array of prospects that, if played out, would be even more unbearable: a kidnapped and murdered child; a child swept away in a storm; a child caught in the wreckage of an automobile.

Dr. Elisabeth Kübler-Ross, writing in a newsletter published for parents who are losing or have lost a child, said,

> Our research in death and life after death has revealed beyond a shadow of a doubt that those [children] who make the transition are more alive, more surrounded with

unconditional love and beauty than you can ever conceive. They are not really dead. They have just preceded us in the evolutionary journey all of us are on; they are with their former playmates—as they call them—or guardian angels; they are with family members who preceded them in death and are unable to miss you as you miss them since they are unable to feel any negative feelings. The only thing that stays with them is the knowledge of love and care that they have received and of the lessons they have learned during their physical life.**

That single paragraph by Dr. Kübler-Ross is particularly profound when you consider her credentials as a medical doctor, psychiatrist, and internationally known thanatologist. She has been studying death and dying for over a quarter of a century from a strictly scientific point of view. Her great body of written work, however, often deals with the spiritual because, she says, she finds that "certain illuminations which I had observed in the mystery of death cannot be explained in strictly scientific language."

In my own experiences involving the death of children, I have had several occasions in which an inexplicable element somehow had to be factored in. One such was the case of a ten-year-old girl who sat watching television with her grandmother one evening and suddenly said, "Ooh, that person is *old*!" The grandmother said simply, "We're all going to get old someday." The little girl said, "No, I'm not. I'm going to die soon."

The grandmother was startled, to say the least, and remarked, "What silly talk. You're still very young. You have many, many years ahead of you."

The strange conversation was only recalled by the grandmother at the little girl's wake. She had died very suddenly shortly after that conversation. When the girl couldn't be awakened one morning, she was rushed to the hospital. She was cold upon arrival and apparently had died sometime during the night. After an especially thorough examination by the resident pathologist, the cause of death was listed as "unknown."

Another girl—a teenager, sixteen—was having dinner with her mother at a rather elegant restaurant after a hectic day of shopping for new school clothes. The mother was tired, but happy with the selections they had made, when the girl said, quite abruptly, "I don't know why we went so overboard. You know I'll never get to wear half of these things, Mother."

The mother was puzzled, of course. "Are there some things you don't like? If that's the case, we can take them back. I don't want you wearing anything you wouldn't feel comfortable and happy in."

"No. I love everything. There aren't many mothers as patient as you are. But," the girl continued, "there are a lot of people I have to see, and I suppose a lot of changes will be fun."

The mother felt the girl was talking very strangely and tried to change the subject. "Have you given any thought to college yet?"

"Oh, it's crossed my mind, but I doubt if I'll ever have to make that choice."

"You'll have to make it when you're a senior in high school…"

"Mother, I haven't got that long."

"Don't act so crazy. You're sixteen!"

"What difference does *that* make?"

The mother was stunned to silence. Certainly the girl needed counseling, yet she was a happy kid, a straight-A student, and had a social life that was remarkable for one so young. She sometimes acted older than her years, but this implication about her impending death was unnerving, to say the least.

Ten nights later, the girl joined a party of several other teenagers to celebrate the end of summer and the start of school. When she left the house, she was unusually loving in her good-nights to her mother and father.

At ten minutes after midnight, her parents received a visit from a village police officer they knew very well. He had tragic news. The car in which their daughter was a passenger, driven by a completely sober and sane young man, had been hit head-on by a drunken driver. All the youngsters survived, except one. Their daughter.

To this day, the mother swears her daughter knew her days were numbered.

Another youngster who suffered from a brain tumor asked me, only days before he died: "Will I continue to grow when I'm in Heaven?"

I couldn't answer him with a definitive "yes" or "no," which is what he was looking for, so instead I asked him, "Do you have a theory about that?"

"Kind of," he said.

"That's very profound thinking for a twelve-year-old. What is your theory?"

"Well, Tchaikovsky obviously had grown up in Heaven. Otherwise, how could he start composing all those complicated symphonies when he was only six or so? He either learned all that before he died or he picked it up in Heaven." The boy and I went down a list of every genius we could think of who arrived on earth with a mind several centuries beyond his or her time.

As stories, these events are quite interesting and intriguing. But they are stories, nonetheless. In my case, they happen to be true, but they are the stuff of which good suspense tales are made, and they abound. The reason we find them so intriguing is that within each story is buried a fragment of mystery that we secretly hope is real.

This I know for a fact: Children know and understand more about death than grownups will ever discover or realize. For example, I believe that God, who created us all, compensates little ones as they fail physically. While they may be weak in body, they become stronger in wisdom and intuitiveness. I have seen it.

I had been visiting a young woman who had been extremely active in our parish, and was known for her tireless work among children. She was an excellent guitarist and singer and almost impossible to beat at tennis. Shortly before she was to become engaged, she developed a polyneuritis which left her weak at first, then finally disabled her. During one of my last visits, she waited until her mother was out of the room, then asked me to take her hand. "I don't know how long I can take this, Father," she said. "I have been fighting the good fight, as they say, but I'm really on the edge. I've been hanging on because of my mother. She has to know, Father, that it's time for me to go. But I almost feel I need her permission. Do you understand?"

I understood. I talked with the mother that evening and explained to her that there comes a time, when life and living is so painful, that the patient would just like to lay back and let God handle the rest. The mother and father had done everything they could. They had brought in every specialist they could find and afford. They tried to give their daughter every comfort, to relieve every hurt and pain. That task was through. They had to face another task—to live on and cherish the memory of this remarkable young woman who had meant so much to them and to all those she had touched.

The mother finally understood. She must let go and let God take care of her daughter.

*The services of the Sudden Infant Death Syndrome Alliance are available to all. For information on SIDS, you may call 1-800-221-SIDS. You will reach the main office of the SIDS Alliance in Columbia, Maryland, which can direct you to affiliations throughout the nation.

**On Children and Death. (New York: Collier Books/ Macmillan Publishing Company, 1985), p. 49.

6

MORE HELP

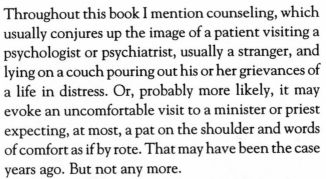

Throughout this book I mention counseling, which usually conjures up the image of a patient visiting a psychologist or psychiatrist, usually a stranger, and lying on a couch pouring out his or her grievances of a life in distress. Or, probably more likely, it may evoke an uncomfortable visit to a minister or priest expecting, at most, a pat on the shoulder and words of comfort as if by rote. That may have been the case years ago. But not any more.

Today there is counseling available for almost every known circumstance or condition, and for just about any type of grief related to loss of any kind. While psychologists and psychiatrists play an important role in treating dysfunction, you are more likely to run into someone just like yourself who has been through a situation almost exactly like your own. These are just "plain folks" who happen to have experienced grief a short while before you did, and know exactly what you're going through. Each has his or her own story, just as you have yours.

To give you an example of how modern-day counseling works and works best, let's take the case of Elaine and Joe Stillwell, founding coleaders of The Compassionate Friends of Rockville Centre, New York.

The Compassionate Friends, an international support group with six hundred chapters, is a self-help organization offering friendship and understanding to bereaved parents and siblings. Participation requires no religious affiliation and no dues. Most local chapters publish a newsletter containing items about picnics, memorials, meetings, and even includes essays and poems.

Elaine's story furnishes some background on the kinds of people who organize such groups. It involves her son, Denis, a twenty-one-year-old lifeguard, ready to enter his junior year at Northeastern University in Boston, studying International Relations; nineteen-year-old Peggy, a county worker who was studying psychology and looking forward to returning to the University of Dayton; and eighteen-year-old Anne, ready to begin her freshman year at Loyola College in Maryland.

Elaine, their mother, was enjoying the summer teaching two classes in the morning and returning each afternoon to Joe, her husband of two years and stepfather of her children. The phone rang constantly, the young people were busy and happy.

The house was full of laughter, teasing, gossip, and dates.

Then one drizzly night in August, the three young people had tickets for an outdoor rock concert at Jones Beach. Anne had to work at her restaurant job that evening and bowed out, as did Denis' girlfriend who had an early work call the next morning. So Denis and Peggy, the inseparables, went together. Although the night was hazy and drizzly with poor visibility, the show went on.

At three-thirty in the morning, Elaine heard the shrill ringing of the telephone, waking her from a deep sleep. She was informed that her son had been in an auto accident and taken to a local hospital. Would she be able to come right away? She asked about Peggy, but nobody seemed to know anything about her. Elaine figured she had met friends at the concert and had left with them. She rationalized that Denis may have a broken arm or leg, but nothing life-threatening crossed her mind. As Elaine and her husband prepared to leave for the hospital, Anne, now awake, wanted to come along, but Elaine asked her to stay home and wait for a call from Peggy.

Fifteen minutes later, Elaine and Joe were in the hospital emergency room and found Denis being prepared for brain surgery. As Elaine looked at this strapping six-foot-three-inch young man, she wondered if he would be well enough to make it back to college next month. The glass cuts on his face had been cleaned and Elaine thought, "Denis can come through anything."

As she signed the papers for Denis' operation, she asked where Peggy was, and the doctor told her Peggy was still at the scene of the accident. Naively, she said, "How silly it was of Peggy to stay and guard Denis' car—his pride and joy—when she should have ridden in the ambulance with him."

The doctor gave her a sympathetic look. "Peggy didn't make it." It took Elaine long minutes to realize that Peggy wasn't with her because she was dead and waiting to be taken to the morgue.

Thus started hours and days of devastation for the Stillwells. Denis, after a long operation, didn't make it either. "In an attempt to keep this tragedy from being in vain, we agreed to donate Denis' tissue and organs to help other people live," Elaine says today. "After the wakes, after the funerals, after the friends and relatives had departed, Joe and I sat in the living room and looked at each other and wondered, 'Where do we begin?' "

It was, at that moment, a terrifying feeling trying to imagine they could go on living. Their pain went to the very core. Elaine said that her heart felt as if it were in a vise. Getting up in the morning took every bit of energy she had. Peggy and Denis haunted every thought. Every bone and muscle in her body ached with real pain.

Through what she called her "stupor of grief," Elaine realized that she had two choices. She could lie down and give up or summon all her strength and attempt to build a meaningful life for her family and herself. "That single thought dragged me out of bed every morning, sent me back to work three weeks after they died, and forced me to fight periodic depression and anger. It helped me put up the Christmas tree, entertain friends, go to weddings, enjoy music. I made the choice to live, and my husband and daughter gave me their support. Joe, whom I call my 'blotter,' helped me dry my tears and gave me the strength that I shared with Annie. Peggy and Denis were vibrant and fun-loving, and we honor them every time we carry out one of their little traditions. We feel better for it because it keeps them alive in our hearts and keeps their memories from being erased.

"After reading every grief book I could get my hands on, I realized that support groups made a difference. I discovered The Compassionate Friends. Because there was no chapter near us, I asked Joe if he would start a local chapter with me. Fourteen months after losing our children, we opened our first TCF chapter. We meet once a month in a local college in our town. We had guessed that we would have ten or, at most, fifteen people at each meeting, but our very first meeting brought out thirty-six bereaved parents! In the past four years, over three hundred families have walked through the doors. Today, attendance ranges between seventy-five and ninety-five people per meeting, with five more families joining us at each succeeding session."

Elaine and Joe believe it is the hand of God at work. They have met "warm, wonderful people who are all hurting terribly, and we have helped to give them hope that they, too, will find joy in their hearts again. We learn to tell our family and friends what we need to survive. They don't automatically know. We learn to do what gives us peace of mind, we learn the activities we can handle and how to surround ourselves with the people who make us feel comfortable. We do a lot of things differently and make new memories, we talk about our children, we thank God for the good old days and live through the tough ones. Helping others actually helps us to heal."

The Compassionate Friends has chapters all over the nation, and very well may have a chapter in your community, but it is only one of the many group counseling services available.

In our area, a funeral home has issued a Bereavement Support Research Directory, which has found great acceptance among families looking for support following the death of a loved one. The directory organizes specific support groups in each category and lists them alphabetically. In the index are such headings as Bereaved Parents, General, Hotline, Hospice, Specialized Groups, Widows and Widowers, and Private Counseling. The contents lists churches of all denominations, church groups, service leagues, outreach programs, hospice care organizations, YM- and YWCAs, YM- and YWHAs, suicide-death groups, sudden infant death syndrome groups, police survivors services, cancer care guidance centers, and many others—most charging no fee. Private counselors generally charge fees, but this is noted in the directory.

Most metropolitan areas have such a directory. If yours does not, I suggest you ask your pastor, your funeral director, or your police department. If you don't feel up to seeking out such support, ask a good friend to do it for you. It will amaze you to find out how completely cooperative people can be. I know of at least one case where the bereaved called the information operator of her local telephone company and was put through immediately to a group that would be able to handle her special need.

As a member of a support group, you will be included in many activities that will give you a completely new start. For example, an organization called The Ray of Hope Foundation conducts seminars all over the country on such subjects as Creative Caregiving, Healing the Holiday Hurts, a Concert of Hope and Healing. There is generally a charge for these seminars, but it is a place where you will meet many people who have been through the very same things you have.

Many large corporations have employee groups that are organized under the banner of "Good Neighbor Funds." It might be appropriate, if you or a family member work for a sizeable firm, to inquire as to the existence of such a help group within the company. Many companies issue pamphlets on such subjects as what to do when a coworker is grieving and how to help at the time of death. They may tell you what to do at work when a member of the staff has suffered the loss of a loved one. There are any number of resources in place that will help the bereaved face such tragedies as suicide, sudden death, accidental death, and homicide.

Almost any hospital public-relations office can direct you to a place for help. Your own doctor most likely has extensive knowledge of help groups.

Town and village telephone directories offer such listings as Widowed Persons Service, Friends of Hospice, Cancer Volunteers of America, Alzheimer's Association, and the AIDS Alliance. It will be quite easy to find the right help group for anyone in bereavement.

7

THE LONG, LONG WAIT

While sudden death and its accompanying shock tears at the heart, perhaps the most grueling, stultifying, wearing kind of vicarious suffering for the parents, the children, or the caregivers of sick loved ones is waiting out the prolonged death. Again, as in any other mortal circumstance, lingering illness is no respecter of age.

Some years ago, before I could easily accept the death of a totally innocent person, I was very close to a couple whose young daughter, Joanne, developed a fatal disorder. At the outset neither her mother nor father suspected anything, except to note that occasionally Joanne would suffer a dizzy spell and fall down. At the age of two and a half Joanne was found to have a brain tumor. Doctors told her mother that it was too deep—inoperable. When the "final" prognosis was made, she and her husband were told that Joanne had only about four months to live.

Joanne's mother remembers leaving the hospital one night and watching the traffic in the street. "Why were things going on so normally—cars speeding by, people hurrying along the sidewalks, laughter, talking—while in another life up in the room behind me there was a tragedy being played out in a child's silence?"

As it happened, another prognosis indicated that the tumor might only begin to affect Joanne's lifestyle in four months, and that people could live for a dozen years after discovering such a malignancy. Could this news be less sad?

There would be many suggestions, theories, trials and errors, in the treatment of Joanne from that time on. One pediatrician found one leg longer than the other and recommended an orthopedic shoe for Joanne to wear, which she did, but not without a great deal of self-consciousness. Another suggested radiation. Still another doctor said no to radiation. But as a test, Joanne went on to cobalt treatments and the tumor shrank.

Her mother remembers the heartbreak of seeing this little child under the giant machine with sandbags across her neck to hold her head in place. The treatments seemed to help, however, so there was a glimmer of hope.

Then there followed the outpatient treatment

she received every six months at a New York clinic.

By the time she was in second grade Joanne was walking and talking quite normally, but then the seizures started again, and new weaknesses appeared—in the eyes, in the limbs. Braces were ordered. Joanne hated them.

In the weeks and months that followed, Joanne's angry, weary, confused, nearly defeated mother was literally on a deathwatch. Her seven-year-old daughter was dying. The long wait nearly wiped the family out financially, but that was never considered a great concern. Then came the crisis, the coma, the bedside wait, the sleepless nights, the phone calls, the silent cacophony of a nightmare, the death, the arrangements, the wake, the funeral, the burial. It all took a tremendous emotional toll on both of Joanne's parents.

Such a long, drawn-out trial puts an enormous strain on one's faith. In this case, the faith of Joanne's parents was strong, and they handled their plight with reason. I heard them express the anger, the questions, the pain, the disbelief, and the guilt they were experiencing. I was honored to be their sounding board. Despite their religious convictions, they may have had questions about God's role in this long siege; but I didn't sense it.

They remember Joanne's birthday every year and commemorate the day of her death, not in any morbid fashion and not with tears, but in the joy they felt during the times when things seemed to be "all right." They share fond memories of her with those who are close to them. They recall funny little anecdotes in a cheerful manner. They adjusted to their bereavement extremely well.

It's normal to wonder where God is during these tragic events. It's a question that is asked sometimes even among the most religious people—those who have received the calling and feel they have the firmest of convictions about God.

A young Jesuit priest in Boston, Father Robert VerEecke, who has ministered to the dying for some years, recently watched lingering death close up. Following a visit to see his dying father in a nursing home on Long Island, he shared his thoughts with his congregation. I asked him to recall some of the words from that Sunday message.

"A few weeks ago," he said, "I gave a homily on playing hide-and-seek with God, but this Sunday the theme has more to do with seeking and *finding*.

"Earlier this week I visited a young man who is dying from AIDS. He wasn't expected to live out the day, and I was called to anoint him. I had seen him two months ago and remembered him as bright and funny—and very much alive. Now, his lifeline was an array of tubes, and he couldn't speak. He could only squeeze my hand in recognition. Like workers in the vineyard, I thought to myself, *This isn't fair! Why someone so young? Why must he suffer so much? Why must his life be lost? Are these really your ways, O God?*"

Then Father VerEecke talked about visiting his father in the nursing home. He celebrated a Mass for his father and a few friends, but he knew his father was completely lost. There was no recognition, except at one moment when his father whispered, "How are you?" But it was spoken to no one in particular. Again, the young priest felt this was so unfair. His father was a man who attended Mass every day of his married life and spent all of his spare time singing in the church choir, as a soloist.

"He deserves more," my friend said. "I asked God, 'Is this how you reward your faithful servants?' My father's life has been reduced to the barest essentials. He eats, sleeps, cries out in pain, and on the rarest occasions speaks a word. My mother's love for him is his lifeline. She will ask him to squeeze her hand, and she will give him a kiss. And he will pucker his lips. Maybe this is all that is keeping him alive—his love for my mother."

In that homily he told of staying at a Cenacle retreat house during the same visit, and celebrating the liturgy for sisters in the infirmary. He says, "As I looked at these sisters, aged and infirm, many in wheelchairs, my heart cried out again: Like those workers in the vineyard, Lord, this is unfair. These women have given their lives to Your service, their lives have been only for Christ. Why must they suffer like this? And then, something very extraordinary happened. As I was giving each sister the body of Christ, a song was playing in the background somewhere. 'I am the bread of life...' and it was at that moment I found what I was seeking. It was this bread of life that was *their* lifeline. For them, life meant Christ. He was there in their pain, in their suffering, giving Himself to them.

"This homily," he said, "was begun in anger and frustration—questioning God, whose ways are not our ways, whose thoughts are not our thoughts. There was this young man with AIDS, my father in the nursing home, these infirm sisters, all of whom seemed to have lost so much of life; and yet for each there was this lifeline, a family's love, my mother's love, the love of Christ himself."

He told me he felt there were no answers to what seems to us to be "unfair" or "undeserved," but if we seek the Lord while He may be found, if we call to Him while He is near, we may find a lifeline that is love itself. His is the divine love of which the Bible speaks. Father VerEecke ended his homily this way: "Our God in Christ is as near as life and death itself. Find the lifeline—and hold on."

My own recent experience with the approach of death after a long illness concerned an old friend named Victor. He had but days, perhaps only hours, when I last visited him. Despite his weakness, he seemed gregarious and circumspect.

When I arrived at his house, he was in the company of his wife, daughter, and the hospice nurse who had been paying him regular visits when he returned home for care.

I smiled and asked, "How are you?"

He smiled back and said, "It's finished. It's over. I'm dying. It's been years."

Victor's wife added, "Three years, Father Tom. The first year was comparatively easy. The last two, very painful for Victor and difficult for all of us."

"Oh, sweetheart," Victor said, his voice soft with care. "What you have been through for me! Honey, I love you more than any person I've ever known. I will never be able to explain how deep my love is for you." A tear started down his cheek. "I'm lonely over the thought that I'm going to be leaving you. But, sweetheart," Victor said, "I'm not trying to run away from you. It's just that God is calling me." He looked at his wife for a minute, then at his daughter, and finally he turned to the nurse. "I'd like to be alone with Father Tom for a few minutes, okay?"

The three women left the room. There was silence while Victor tried to phrase his question properly and succinctly. "Father, am I dying because I'm just plain tired or is it because of God's will?"

I looked into his face which now wore a look of pleading, urgency, and pain. I said, "Victor, your wife and daughter love you very much. In all these years, you probably never really knew *how* much. Believe me when I say God is calling you, Victor. Your wife and daughter know that, too, and they will be relieved to know that as their care comes to an end, there will be someone else to care for and love you until the three of you are together again. Now, Victor, I'm going to anoint you. You will go to God in peace."

Victor smiled. "Isn't that wonderful! Yes, by all means, Father, anoint me, please." The next night, Victor left us in his sleep.

It's almost impossible to imagine how patients must have suffered both physically and emotionally during long terminal illnesses before the advent of our modern medicines and compassionate health care. But even today, conventional treatment revolves around two extremes. There is the attitude that "nothing further can be done," opposed by a frantic effort to "do something" for the dying patient.

Western culture has evolved to view death as something to be feared, rather than to see death as a mystery to be trustfully entered. Thanatologists tell us that death is often viewed as an enemy. The experience of dying has been changed from one that is spiritual, communal, and comfortable, to one that is institutional and distant. Hospice care has been a great part of the answer to the question, "How can we help the dying?" But there still is some confusion about what hospice care really is.

Hospice is a medically directed multidisciplinary program that provides skilled care for terminally ill patients *and* their families. Hospice care helps patients and their families live as fully as possible until the time of death; helps relieve symptoms of discomfort;

and provides support in the times of distress that may occur during the course of the disease, dying, and bereavement. This distress can take many forms—physical, psychological, spiritual, social, and even economic.

Our expert on the subject is Jeanne Towers, a nurse on a hospice unit for ten years, an inspirational speaker, and a leader in the hospice philosophy. Jeanne recalls a patient named Eileen whose cancer had spread from the breast to her bones and spinal column, leaving her almost completely paralyzed and totally dependent on others for her physical needs.

"Eileen's husband was most anxious to take her home," Jeanne relates. "Her home care was arranged with visiting nurses and volunteers. The family, which included two teenage daughters, looked forward to her return home. The evening prior was Eileen's birthday, and we had a party for her. Other patients and their visiting families joined the celebration, and the next morning we found a note, painstakingly written, which read in part: 'Thank you for being such a beautiful part of my day, and bringing me such happiness.'

"I will always remember how pleased Eileen was that day and how she showed such strength," Jeanne recalls. "Three weeks later she died peacefully at home with her family around her."

Hospice workers feel that there is a philosophy to be embraced if we are ever to begin to overcome unrealistic attitudes to the normal process of dying.

The word *hospice* can be traced back to medieval Europe when it meant a way station, a refuge, a place where pilgrims could stop off and be refreshed before continuing their journey.

Today, since the creation of hospices in the late sixties in England, the word refers to a specialized health care program designed to help people with terminal illness live with a pleasant, dignified quality of life right up until the moment of death. There is a National Hospice Organization, established in 1980, which has set up guidelines for hospice care. This organization recognizes the physical, emotional, and spiritual well-being of both patient and family caregivers, enabling the patient to progress through his or her illness and still maintain as much control and dignity as is the patient's basic human right. Hospice programs are supported by government agencies as well as through volunteer fund-raising activities. Each hospice unit has a dedicated team of professional physicians, nurses, social workers, home health aides, dietitians, and nonmedical volunteers.

By way of example, Jeanne recalls a patient named Vincent who, on his initial interview for admission to hospice, "had so much tubing coming out of every orifice that I had to literally follow each line and determine its purpose. He had come to our unit from a large metropolitan hospital with the prognosis that nothing more could be done. He made very little eye contact, and stared out the window whenever nursing care was necessary. Often he didn't even open his eyes or acknowledge our presence, feigning sleep.

"One dark, dreary rainy morning," Jeanne remembers, "I entered the room and found Vincent in his usual mute mood with his flat expression and I commented on the rain—insignificant talk about the weather. No response. His stillness was unsettling. A while later, after carefully assisting him out of his bed and into a chair, I sat down and asked him how he felt about having to function with all of those tubes connected to him. Softly, one word at a time, he told me all about the progression of his illness and what it had been like during the major surgeries he had been through. He didn't want to live the rest of his life, no matter how short a time that might be, with all the tubes serving his daily functions.

"I just listened for a while, and then after a moment, I thought about my earlier try at conversation about the rain. Then Vincent said, 'I heard you and I thought about how bothered I would be about bad weather if I had to travel to work like you, or if I had to go some place on vacation. But now, all that doesn't matter. Rain or shine, each day is a gift now and the day itself has meaning regardless of the weather.'

"Vincent got to go home, and as was his wish, the tubes were disconnected one by one. He began eating and gaining some weight. His disease went into a stage of remission, something the doctors had never thought possible. Vincent lived another year and a half—eighteen months more in which he saw his daughter married. He died at home with his wife and family by his side."

If the long difficult wait has any "up" side, it is this: There is time to prepare for a period of bereavement. This may sound morbid at first, but giving some thought to what will surely become a highly emotional experience is not out of line. The professional caregivers in a hospice unit, for example, can be extremely helpful in finding you counseling in advance. There are many large crises you will face, because grief follows no standard timetable or set of rules. You must learn to be patient with yourself. You will face depression and anger, you may find yourself unable to concentrate and unwilling to get back into life's routines. If you are a friend or relative of the person who is about to face bereavement, association with a counseling group might help you understand what your friend or relative will be going through and be able to encourage that person to find help. You will be more sensitive to the changes in the experiences of a bereaved family. You will learn to stay in touch with the family, because grief does not end at the close of the funeral service. You will learn to avoid judgments of any kind, and you will learn how to offer real help rather than just the tired, usual offer: "If there's anything I can do, let me know."

Being a proper support to someone in bereavement is probably the most important friendship role you will ever play.

8

THE FEARFUL THOUGHT

At a wake I recently attended, I overheard a man—perhaps in his fifties—nod to the bier and say, "That'll be me in twenty years." It was a solemn statement, and started me thinking about the problems of people who have a genuine fear of death.

Unless that fear is somehow dampened or eliminated, it can do serious harm. Watching people in this dilemma often brings to mind a friend of mine who was a singer with the big bands of the forties and fifties. Once while I was visiting him, he showed me a few of his hits—some of them are still being played on the air. They have become "standards." His rise to stardom was swift, the kind of upward sweep that some of his peers experienced—people like Frank Sinatra, Bob Eberle, and Dick Haymes.

As many people in the entertainment business

can testify, sudden fame can be hard to handle. The personality is in the spotlight almost overnight; he is being applauded and adored by thousands of people he has never met. He is living on cloud nine, yet he still carries a lot of baggage from the days when he was an unknown, struggling young vocalist with barely a dollar in his pocket, and finding rejection all around.

Shortly after my friend's first hit record, his cousin died suddenly of congestive heart failure. He was a celebrity at the wake, a situation that caught him off guard. The morning of the funeral, he found his heart pounding rapidly and cold sweat appearing on his brow. He felt uneasy and slightly dizzy. He sat on the edge of the bed for a while waiting for the sensation to pass, but it wouldn't go away. His mother offered him aspirin, then one of her own tranquilizers. By the time the limousine had arrived to take them to the church, he was feeling much better, but the mystery of that little setback bothered him.

After the funeral there was plenty to eat and plenty to drink—especially to drink. After a couple of martinis my friend wondered why that little dizzy spell had upset him at all.

A couple of days later while he was riding in a cab in New York, he had a similar sensation—dizziness and a fear that he was losing control of himself. He asked the driver to stop and he got out of the cab, gasping for air.

At that time, a trip to the doctor hadn't even crossed his mind. He just had a couple little "spells." He was to discover as time passed, and the so-called spells recurred, that if he stopped for a quick drink, the feeling of well-being would return. While his few minutes in a bar were great fun, he was careful never to carry his drinking habits to work with him.

One night just before a show in Chicago, my friend had the feeling that he couldn't possibly go on. His heart was pounding again and he felt as if he wanted to run out the stage door screaming.

This time he confided in the pianist, who quickly diagnosed his condition as a hangover and handed him a couple of heavy-duty tranquilizers. That did the trick for that evening. He did go on, and he didn't fall off the stage as he had actually feared.

When he got back to New York he paid a visit to his doctor, who gave him a complete physical and ordered extensive tests. "We can't let anything happen to you at the height of your success," the doctor said. My friend the singer was relieved when all of his tests came back negative. After all, he was only twenty-eight at the time and hadn't really abused his body.

My friend and I discussed this some years later as he was about to retire from the music business. I was amazed to find out how long it took and how much he suffered before anyone could figure out the answer to his problem.

"I think my cousin Gregory's death triggered

it," he told me, "but I'm not sure. My therapist drew me a picture of what the problem could be. By then I was almost a wreck. I had gagging and coughing spells at the most awkward times, I still got dizzy spells, I still thought I was going to lose control, that I was going to fall down and embarrass myself in front of other people. A few drinks would put it out of my mind and sometimes phenobarbital seemed to help, but the doctors were just treating the symptoms. Then I heard an analysis that made sense, and my shrink explained it to me much like he would explain a children's story to a kid.

"He said that long ago, before man had invented the rifle, or even the bow and arrow, he had a terrific problem with wild animals. If he found himself in the jungle or forest with no means of combat, and heard a lion's roar, the 'chemical set' in his body would take over. His heartbeat would increase, the adrenaline would start pumping, and sugar would be rushed into his bloodstream. In that instant, the man in the jungle was ready to run—to run for his life. What had happened was this: The man heard the roar and immediately had a fearful thought. His brain reacted instantly and he literally raced away from the scene.

"Today we still have fearful thoughts, and they manifest themselves in the same way. They trigger the same thing that the man in the forest felt: Panic. Human beings have had panic attacks since God gave them a sense of fear, but in today's civilization, there's no place to run. You can't run in a cab. You can't run away when you're performing a song. People would think you were crazy, and *that* thought enters the mix too."

I had heard this theory expressed more than once in conversations with doctors and psychologists, and it sounded fairly rational to me, so the next question to my friend the singer was obvious: "What was your fearful thought? What flashed through your mind that caused all these attacks?"

He looked at me, shook his head as if to clear it, leaned back in his chair, and said calmly, "I was afraid of death. I was afraid I was going to die."

"Why?"

"I don't know. But whenever I wasn't *doing* something, whenever I was just sitting, reclining, or waiting for something, I would dwell on my own death. When would it be? How would it be? What would bring me down? Would it happen when I was doing so well? Would it spoil my success? What would I miss? Ah ha! that was the big question. What would I miss? Would all the people I know keep going—seeing, hearing, laughing, singing—when I died? Would I die a lonely death? Who would really care?"

"How did you beat it?" I asked him.

"Well, first of all, I thought I had found out what it was, but I wasn't really sure. I thought back over all the hell I had been through and hoped to God that I had found the loose screw in my brain.

When I explained this to my shrink, he said that death, a wake, or a funeral could certainly set off such a domino effect. But being a doctor with some sense, he wouldn't declare it a complete victory right away. The last thing he said to me was, 'I can't convince you that there is nothing medically the matter with you. The only way you can be sure I'm telling you the right thing is to look back at this visit thirty years from now and say—gee, nothing happened to me. I didn't die, after all!' "

A phobia can be anything from a nuisance to a full-blown psychosis, and the fear of death can often be paralyzing because we are all aware that it will come to us sooner or later. My friend the singer may have been sorry that his cousin died, but nowhere during our conversation did he indicate grief. Instead, like the man who said, "In twenty years that will be me," he was creating a case for his own mortality and the case he built was one he found unpleasant, and it was reflected in his very physical being. In fact, it almost ruined his life.

We must be aware of some ramifications of real grief too. Doctors with whom I associate at St. Francis Hospital on Long Island and in other medical centers can point to many reactions to grief that we should be aware of.

Grief can vary with the personality of the individual. In most cases there is a general sense of uneasiness or discomfort. This is normal and certainly not serious. Some people react with shaking and tremors, and occasionally the muscles in the legs, arms, and hands don't react properly. While this condition usually resolves itself in a matter of hours, it can be alarming.

The glandular system may be activated, too, and the mourner may experience dryness of the mouth, or the tear ducts may overflow. It is possible that a person suffering from acute grief can be more vulnerable to infections and viral illnesses. Grief may trigger high blood pressure as well as changes in the body temperature, cold chills, and hot flashes. The variations in physical reactions depend on the person.

What bothers most of us about grief is that it brings with it certain emotional manifestations. We feel sorrow, and we find ourselves with fears, anxiety, and uncertainty about the future. Unless we are party to a lingering illness in which there is time to get all affairs in order, to make specific plans for the future, a spouse or child may suddenly feel lost. The closer the human relationship, and the more sudden the death, the deeper the feeling of helplessness.

Is there any way to avoid the fearful thought or any way to prepare to meet grief situations? I know it is a great deal to ask when the world's media and educational institutions are so full of wonderful distractions. But if the thought of death bothers you, or if someone close to you is in the process of dying, you could do worse than courageously study the subject. Your public library can supply you with any number of readable books on the subject. There are high school and college courses that can give you an in-depth clinical study of the mysteries of life and death.

Then there is what we in the clergy call a *philosophy of life*. We probably first heard this phrase in elementary school, but have only a vague idea of what it means. As we grow older, we may still not have a clear idea of how we view life, what life should be like, or how we can help make it as right as possible for ourselves and others. We probably avoid it because the very thought of having a solid philosophy frightens us.

As a priest, I had to develop one within the tenets of my Church. Actually, it's quite simple—a short list of how we feel about certain things. For example:

- What, in your mind, is the difference between good and evil?
- Can you define love?
- Do you help others, or do you merely believe that someone should help others?
- How do you feel about monogamy?
- What does it take to be an honest person?
- Do you believe in God?
- Do you believe you have a responsibility toward God?
- Do you feel that God has a responsibility toward you?

- Can you define serenity and happiness?
- What is death?

These are but a few items on the list, and our philosophy of life is created by how we perceive the answers to these very broad questions. If you know about something, have studied it, and have formed an opinion about it, that, then, is your philosophy. You will be able to work through grief more readily if you have a philosophy of life *and* of death.

9

WHY A WAKE?

Among Protestant and Roman Catholic families, the wake is a rather traditional event before the funeral. The wake is a vigil period of waiting for the funeral itself. Some time ago wakes were held in the family home. It was an occasion for neighbors and relatives to visit and to sustain the family in its grief, and to pay respect to the body of the deceased. It was also a time when survivors joined together in an expression of faith.

Over the years, the wake has become a more organized ritual, most often conducted in the funeral home during prearranged hours that are convenient for those who are expected to attend. The local parish or church usually provides a prayer service at a designated hour during the course of the wake which will include Scripture readings and meditative responses. In the case of a Catholic wake, the priest may invite the family to select the readings. The saying of the rosary is still observed in some places. The family chooses whether the casket is to remain open or closed.

Various ministers and priests handle the service at the wake in their own particular manner. In my case, I pray en route to the wake, asking that I will be able to get out of God's way when I appear. *How* I appear when I arrive at the funeral home is also important, I feel. Of course I will be in clerical dress, but that is only the facade. I must be the personification of affirmation, for the priest is the emissary of Christ. I represent Him and I must administer as He would. I take this mandate very seriously because upon arrival I generally find distraught family members and a roomful of people who are quite uncomfortable. There's an uneasiness—friends who don't know exactly what to do or say. Everyone is looking for an answer, a perspective, and hope.

Mourners and sympathizers perceive a wake as a sacred time, and in most respects it is, but I believe it is also a time for relationships as well as Scripture reading and prayer. Christ was compassionate and merciful. He went out of His way to help the bereaved, people in trouble, people who were hungry, people who were in pain. When Christ was on earth, He introduced all people to the love of God and helped alleviate the pain and sorrow. That is my role at the wake.

Over the years I have noticed two kinds of pain

and hurt. One is the hurt of love—the hurt you feel when you mourn someone you deeply loved and who gave your life meaning and dimension. The other hurt is the pain you feel when you sense the person who has died had a misspent life. It is up to me to be aware of the difference, to be aware of what's happening in the room.

No two circumstances will be exactly alike. The grief might be for a young man or woman taken in sudden death leaving spouse or children; an accident victim; a grandparent who died after a long illness; a murdered child. Some deaths are so painful, so crippling, because the loved ones didn't even have a chance to say good-bye.

So here I am. The priest at the wake. Perhaps I knew the deceased very well. I may have attended her baptism, his wedding, or an anniversary. It might be someone from my first parish, or a close and dear friend of many years. Perhaps I am simply the priest-called-in who doesn't know the deceased at all. Whatever the situation, I am here and I must build a bridge between earth and Heaven.

I open my Bible and look for Scripture passages that closely fit the experience of these people who are gathered to mourn and show their respect. Sometimes I start with Matthew 7:7—"Ask, and it will be given you; search, and you will find; knock, and the door will be opened for you."

Or I may choose John 14:1-7:

"Do not let your hearts be troubled. Believe in God, believe also in me. In my Father's house there are many dwelling places. If it were so, would I have told you that I go to prepare a place for you? And if I go and prepare a place for you, I will come again and will take you to myself, so that where I am, there you may be also. And you know the way to the place where I am going." Thomas said to him, "Lord, we do not know where you are going. How can we know the way?" Jesus said to him, "I am the way, and the truth, and the life. No one comes to the Father except through me. If you know me, you will know my Father also. From now on you do know him and have seen him."

I talk with the people assembled about the love of God the way Jesus did. I want them to know there is a life after death, that God who gave us this life will give us life there.

Three things I feel important to remember:

• The family needs support now and will need more support when the house becomes silent and the memories begin to flood. This is when they will need a real friend. It is a tribute to the deceased to care for his or her family and friends.

- The most profound thing you can do is to pray for them—talk to God about them. I believe that those who have died are still connected, us to them and them to us.
- Turn to the clergy and other pastoral caregivers, and be open to professional counseling if grief seems overwhelming.

I often wait until the end of the wake and then ask members of the family to sit with me in a circle. In this more intimate setting, we talk about the Mass of the Resurrection that will be celebrated the next day. I explain that I will be wearing white—a symbol of joy—and I quickly go through the details of the funeral Mass. Then I ask for their help. Can they tell me about the person who died? What are some of the stories they remember? What was outstanding about this person? What will they, the family and friends, remember? Then, "Would any of you like to speak at the funeral? Would any of you like to bring up the gifts? Besides the chalice and paten, is there anything you'd like to bring up that would remind you of the loved one?"

At the funeral, I've seen the youngest child bring up a baseball, a teenager bring up a model airplane Grandpa made, and once a small girl brought up a fishing rod. People recalling special moments. At the altar, a wife reminds her husband's relatives and friends of how he got his nickname, a husband tells of his wife's fine works. The purpose is to find out from the family what people should know about their loved one's life so that pertinent memories might be highlighted during the ceremony.

Finally, I invite the family to call me in the morning before the funeral with any special requests, or if I can't be reached, I encourage them to come see me before the service.

There is something else I try to do when I leave the wake—give people a hug. It may sound trivial, but death is so profound and emotions run so high that mourners are looking for something or someone to hold on to. And as I leave, I realize that some may not believe, but I will know that *they* believe that *I* believe. Then I will have done God's work.

In planning the wake the family should consider the purpose of the wake and the needs of relatives and friends. The wake is a preparation for the funeral and should not be so elaborate as to make the funeral itself anticlimatic. I happen to believe that a certain informality that might be inappropriate at the funeral Mass would be entirely appropriate at the wake, depending of course on who and what the deceased represents.

The funeral is a service of prayer which, in the Catholic faith, is usually incorporated in the celebration of the funeral Mass. The casket is covered with a white pall, symbolic of the white robe of baptism. The priest himself wears white vestments, emphasizing the joy of faith that overcomes the sadness of death.

After the opening statement, the body is brought to the head of the church near the altar. The paschal candle—a sign of Christ through baptism—is placed at the casket. A Liturgy of the Word follows the opening prayer with readings from the Bible. As I explained earlier, relatives and friends of the deceased are encouraged to select readings and to offer them from the pulpit. The priest then delivers a homily. The Liturgy of the Eucharist follows, with gifts of bread and wine brought forth and the eucharistic prayer proclaimed. This prayer includes several acclamations for the people and incorporates a narration of the Last Supper, a memorial of Christ's death and resurrection, calling upon the Holy Spirit, and an offering of the sacrifice. The communion follows, with the Lord's Prayer and the reception of the Eucharist. After communion, the Rite of Commendation (a special set of prayers commending the deceased to God's mercy and love) concludes the funeral Mass.

The Jewish funeral, on the other hand, is unique. There are no two services exactly alike. As soon as possible after the moment of death, the survivors are urged to call their rabbi. If the family has little or no relationship with a rabbi or synagogue, the funeral director should be contacted for referral. The rabbi will help plan the funeral service.

The Jewish funeral is a rite of separation. The presence of a casket actualizes the experience. The funeral affords an opportunity for the community to offer support and share sorrow. The rabbi will recite those prayers which are expressive of the spirit of Judaism, the memory of the deceased, and the hope for life in the world to come.

The most commonly used reading is Psalm 23, which expresses the faith of the members of the flock in the justice of the divine Shepherd. From the Psalms, "I lift my eyes to the mountain; whence shall help come to me? My help is from the Lord, who made heaven and earth." During the recitation of the prayer *El Molay Rahamin*, the Hebrew name of the deceased is mentioned. The eulogy of the dead is usually included in the service to recognize not only that a death has occurred but that a life has been lived.

Unlike many other religions, the Jewish burial usually takes place within a day or two after death. Thus, the bereaved have immediate and pressing concerns in the arrangement of the funeral.

It is generally inappropriate to visit the bereaved family between the time of death and the time of the funeral. One pays respect to the deceased by attending the funeral service and then by offering condolences by visiting the home during the mourning period which extends through the first week after burial. The most appreciated expression of condolence is one's presence at both the funeral and the house of bereavement.

The mourning period at the home is called Shiva. The prophet Ezekiel affirms that the mourner should be able to "sigh in silence." Pleasantries at the Shiva are not considered appropriate. The question is often asked, "What can one bring to the house of bereavement?" Material gifts are small solace, but bringing food, "the meal of condolence," is always considered acceptable. As for flowers, many Jews regard the use of flowers as pagan and discourage their use. Often the obituary will carry a line that reads: "In lieu of flowers, contributions may be made to [the synagogue, or a hospital, or some specified charity]."

Jewish people pray to the God of Abraham, the God of Isaac, and the God of Jacob, but each has to find God in his or her own way. In Judaism, death is both real and inescapable—organic, natural, and a logical part of life.

Judaism has always believed in life after death, although Bible references are sparce.

The Orthodox Jew is committed to a belief in physical resurrection of the body at the end of time. Other movements in Judaism may or may not share this view, but its remoteness makes it less central to their teachings. So even within the three Jewish movements—Reformed, Orthodox, and Conservative—there is wide latitude yet some similarity in thought.

10

WHAT DOES THE UNDERTAKER UNDERTAKE?

Most people think they know what a mortician does; but I'm frequently surprised, if not dismayed, by how little many people *really* know about the person who is in charge of the deceased.

For this book I took a rather unusual step for me. I called a mortician whom I have known over the years, and whose service to the community stretches back generations—a man named George Dalton—who serves thousands of families on Long Island with four funeral homes. Highly respected in his field, George is a past president of the New York State Funeral Directors Association and has often been lauded for both his business acumen and his innate compassion for the families that come to him.

I asked him some very obvious, and some not-so-obvious, questions about the role of the undertaker in a family crisis.

A century ago an undertaker was depicted in stories as an ancient, gnarled man in a high black hat and a long black cape, symbolic of his "dealing with the dead." Not today. He is probably a very active member of one or more civic clubs and is the first person asked for donations to all charitable and civic causes, which is why his logotype appears on everything from church bulletins to school programs.

My questions to George, I felt, could be helpful for anyone who has never been in the position of handling a wake, a funeral, or a burial.

First, there is no difference between funeral directors, morticians, or undertakers. They are persons educated and trained to prepare human bodies for funeral and burial. Most, not all, are licensed embalmers. Those who are not, use the services of a local embalming service. All states license morticians, and each state requires specific courses in the procedure. Likewise, there is no real difference between funeral homes, mortuaries, or memorial homes. These are generally the premises where care and preparation of the deceased are provided. Rooms and special areas are provided for the viewing by the bereaved, and arrangements are made for visitation, wakes, and funeral services with the accompanying rites or ceremonies.

After being selected by the family to serve

them, the funeral director removes or arranges for the removal of the deceased to the funeral home. Information for the death certificate and obituary notice is secured as early as is convenient for the family. It is the funeral director who is responsible for the proper completion and *filing* of the death certificate, at which time the burial or transit permit is secured. This is one of the duties often unrealized and misunderstood by the survivors, but is a necessary and vital action that is now part of what the undertaker "undertakes." Whatever the obituary says about the deceased is entirely up to the survivors. Details of a business career or of outstanding community or military service can be given to the mortician and included in the newspaper report. However, the mortician is not a personal press agent, so he or she can submit only the information received. The mortician will also keep the obituary as brief as the survivors wish.

The funeral director also makes an appointment to discuss the various phases of the service. These include church or funeral home, the time of the service, and the person who will officiate at the funeral, to be certain that all details of the wake, funeral, and interment occur on schedule and without misunderstanding or mishap.

During these hectic hours, the funeral director will ask the survivors—generally the spouse or next of kin—to select a casket from a showroom devoted exclusively to a display of many kinds at varied prices. After the selection of a casket, the funeral director will discuss the specific arrangements the family desires. The family will be presented with an itemized list in which every detail of the funeral arrangement is described. When the family or the survivor has decided exactly what services are desired—memorial items, hairdressing, embalming, restoration, use of facilities for visitation, clothing, automobile expense, to name a few—the funeral director will list the cost of each service on every line. By law, there can be no hidden costs. Line-item costs are closely supervised by the Bureau of Funeral Direction in every state. Not only does the mortician have to supply the family with item-by-item costs, but an exact duplicate of the bill of sale must be prepared for state inspectors. It cannot even be a carbon copy of what the funeral director gives the family.

Generally incorporated in the service a mortician offers is the hearse and the use of funeral cars—usually limousines—for members of the family. The funeral director will arrange to pick up the family members on the day of the funeral and engage these same vehicles for the trip to the cemetery and the return.

On the day of the services, which may be one, two, three, or more days from the time of death, the funeral director attends to the floral arrangements, arranges for the physical facilities, organizes the funeral cortege, briefs the ushers and casket bearers, and in some instances makes a car available to carry flowers to the cemetery. Sometimes there are further items dictated by a particular service. Occasionally, the family's wishes and desires will modify some of the details, but experienced funeral directors will handle any special request with ease. This is not new to them.

An item seldom considered or even known about during the duress of the wake and funeral is the service the mortician provides after the ceremony is over. The funeral director assists the family in filing necessary claims for Social Security, veterans and union benefits, and insurance. Sometimes the funeral director serves a family for weeks and months until all matters and details are satisfactorily completed.

In any event, you will know exactly what you are getting and exactly what you are paying for with every part of the funeral director's service, and the law is strictly enforced. Of course, prices vary with each funeral director, depending on the cost of providing services in the area in which you live.

The funeral director can also assist in the selection of a cemetery plot, breaking ground, providing a canopy and other such services at the burial site. If the death is sudden and no thought has been given to the burial site, the funeral director can be a valued consultant. He knows the workings of every cemetery in his area and can guide you on locations, costs, and other details, such as the cemetery's reputation, upkeep, and access.

Advertisements by cemeteries urge people to select plots or vaults long before their use is ever considered. In most instances, this is a good idea. Many people wait until the death of a loved one before selecting a cemetery and plot—but it may be wiser to make the choice well ahead. For example, there comes a time when a family plot might be considered in a specific cemetery. This planning should be done well in advance to be certain that there is room in a place where the selection is satisfactory. This does not have to be a gruesome chore. On the contrary, when plots are purchased in advance, it is comforting for the survivors to know that there is one less important decision to be made. It also expedites the handling of many details at the time of the wake and funeral.

Today, many seniors are also considering paying for their own funerals in advance to save the survivors the worry and work of all the preparations and details. However, this is something to be discussed directly with the funeral director because federal and state laws are involved.

Let's say an aging gentleman who is comparatively well-off decides to prepay his funeral so that he can have everything exactly the way he wants it. The government realizes that there is a possibility that he might spend the last several months of his life in a hospital or a nursing home, and that the costs could leave the patient penniless.

Section 1613(d) of the Social Security Act

provides for an exclusion from resource limits of certain, separately identifiable, funds set aside for burial expenses, with a maximum initial value of fifteen hundred dollars for one person. These funds are not to be commingled with nonburial funds. This burial fund exemption may include any, or a combination of, bank accounts, stocks, bonds, life insurance and/or a prepaid burial agreement. These details are spelled out to nursing homes and hospitals.

Therefore, someone who wishes to prepay a funeral will find there are only certain items for which a funeral director can accept advance payment. These include the casket, crypt, cost of opening and closing the gravesite, headstone, and mausoleum or other repository for remains. The advantage in prepaying is that you can spend more on these items than would be covered by a flat fee of fifteen hunded dollars. That amount could then be added to the cost of the funeral services. For example, you might want an expensive casket and certain special arrangements. However, there are some items you *cannot* prepay: chapel, clergy, honorariums, clothing or burial garments, hearse, limousine, newspaper notices, pallbearers, transcripts, transfer of remains to the funeral chapel, special arrangements and facilities, and some other services. All of this will be explained in detail by your funeral director should you be contemplating such plans.

There is no one prescribed form for the funeral. Religious and personal beliefs, standards and lifestyles are involved. Funeral practices differ even within the United States. What is conventional in New York may be strange in Minnesota. A New Orleans funeral and method of disposition would be greatly different from a service in, say, Utah.

Of equal note is the variance between a Jewish Shiva and an Irish wake being held practically next door to each other.

I have never come in contact with a funeral home in my own area that had any reputation of overpricing, not completing any services paid for, or not being extremely sensitive to the needs, tastes, and desires of its clients. Of course, there are a very few who might take advantage of the gravity of the situation and the vulnerability of the survivors, particularly when the death is sudden and the survivors are in obvious shock. As in any other business, such licensed funeral directors can be reported, investigated, and in some instances, lose their right to practice. Always ask for a detailed price list as described above. It must be prepared for you by law.

I have often felt one had to be a very special person to be able to handle the demanding task of a funeral director. There is one item which is not on the list and can bear no price tag: the compassion the funeral director has for the bereaved and the way in which the mortician and staff conduct the arrangements. Tact and sensitivity to the survivors are the most important requirements, and it would be wise to ask your clergy person or even close friends who know of the funeral home to advise you, particularly on this point.

If that's generally what a funeral director or mortician does, what is the role of the coroner?

The coroner is an elected official of the county whose primary concern is the investigation of sudden deaths as to whether or not there were questionable circumstances. The coroner needs no specific qualifications for the post; many are funeral directors, some are physicians, some are simply politicians. If the deceased is at home at the time of expiration, the coroner is never notified unless something about the death might be considered unusual or suspicious.

Who is the medical examiner? He or she is an appointed official at the city, county, or state level. He or she must be a physician and, in almost all jurisdictions today, must be a trained pathologist— one who has acquired additional formal training in the performance of autopsies and investigations in certain kinds of cases such as sudden, suspicious, violent, unexpected, unexplained, and medically unattended deaths.

You will never have to worry about contacting either the coroner or the medical examiner. The hospital, police, or funeral director will do it for you as a matter of course. The funeral director is also very well versed in the work of both the coroner and the medical examiner so your involvement as a survivor is minimal, except perhaps to provide any special information that might be helpful in determining the cause of death.

This is just about all you will ever have to know about these particular services. The best advice is: Put your problems into the hands of someone who is a specialist and knows exactly how to lighten your burden. But check details first.

11

GOING
THROUGH IT

"I just can't go through it!"

How many times have you thought that? Said that? Told that to others? To paraphrase an old bromide: "You can't go over it, you can't go around it, you can't crawl under it. The only thing you can do is open the door and go through it." You will find, I think, when you accept that resolve, your journey will be shorter than you imagined.

Grief is tough. No question about it. But still you feel that caring for yourself after the death of a husband or wife will change things so dramatically that you may not be able to cope.

So let's examine where you are. You've suffered the shock. You have dealt with—or realized you're dealing with—denial. You have already faced some extremely difficult decisions, because the fact of the matter is irrefutable. You had to face selecting a mortuary, deciding on a casket, deciding whether to have a wake, where it should be, and at what time. You have dealt with the gravesite, and you have made endless phone calls—all, really, within a matter of hours.

You probably haven't really had time to grieve. But grieve you will.

There's an old platitude that says, "Grief is a private matter."

Well, yes and no. To think that nobody can help you during a period of bereavement is not true. Your grief does not have to be a private matter, nor for your own good should it be. You need other people as much or more than you ever needed them before. You have to talk about your feelings and listen to others as they share your bereavement. It is my experience that there is a lot of comfort in sharing, and if you will not or cannot share, you could be doing yourself some emotional, even physical, harm. Sharing can give you the strength to endure your bereavement. Sharing can help you let go of the thoughts that seem to be crushing your soul. In such sharing, others will demonstrate that you weren't the first person to face this difficult time nor will you be the last.

Most of all, sharing will give you the chance to express yourself, to tell little meaningful things to others, and have others commiserate or even empathize.

In this context we're talking about close friends, neighbors, and even business associates. You can find support in many places: From members of your bridge club, your bowling league, the organizations you belong to, and certainly your church or synagogue. Many churches have support groups—sensitive and caring people who seem to know instinctively the right words to say to someone who is newly bereaved.

At first you may hesitate to find a group. The very word *group* seems to signify a certain formality, a sort of "meeting situation," and you may have certain aversions toward meetings of any kind. But I can assure you a support group is nothing like any "meeting" you ever attended. You will be associating with people just like you, people who have been through the very things you are going through now. The more "social" your grief is, the more you talk about it away from your home, the more you share in the grief of others, the more effectively you will adapt to your own loss.

Another fear a bereaved person may harbor is the fear of having to keep up a happy facade, that somehow crying is demeaning in the company of others, that it is a personal imposition on others' feelings. Wrong. No one with an ounce of compassion finds tears inappropriate.

When do you begin to share? At the first moment of shock or loss. The very second you feel that nobody else can help you and you feel you will find yourself carrying the burden of grief alone, turn to others. If you think about it, that's why they're there. There may be one or two or three or maybe a hundred. They are there for *you*.

There is a myth that men have more difficulty sharing grief experiences than women. That attitude is as fictional as the books and movies that allow the woman to weep, but never the strong man. There may have been a time when men felt that tears were a sign of weakness, and that sharing tough emotional times with others was out of the question; but that hasn't been my experience since I have been in the priesthood.

Men do cry. I cry. We all cry. It's good for us. It's a cleansing. Weeping is a merciful release that is built into our chemistry, just the way shock absorbers are built into our systems. If we couldn't fend off shock, and if we couldn't cry, what would we do? No one laughs when someone cries.

When I counsel individuals who have lost family members or friends, I try to convince them that there is such a thing as healthy grief, and that it is, indeed, a journey, a seemingly dark, rocky path. And invariably as I walk this journey with them I see, step by step, that they are making it, and step by step they are finding themselves equal to the challenge.

A parishioner of mine, a woman in her late fifties, with many healthy years ahead of her, seemed to be destroyed by the sudden loss of her husband who was only two years her senior. What would she do? Would she ever be able to go out in the world again? What would her lonely life be like without him?

At first, the woman didn't see the people around her. Her mind blocked out her grown children, her brothers and sisters, her friends and neighbors. She felt she was walking through a dark tunnel, afraid to rest in the bed she had shared with her life partner these many years. Then, gradually, as she moved through her imaginary tunnel, she became aware of human forms. She grew accustomed to the dimness, the forms became clear, and she was able to hear the voices of all the people she loved most.

She was not alone after all. She was even aware of the spirit of her husband in the conversations with her family, in the reminders left around the house. As her faith began to shine through, she knew she would be all right. She could handle her own grief.

I might add this: Your grief is real and must be dealt with. You must not be embarrassed by it. Some people are, but I attribute that to shyness and the desire not to be an emotional burden to anyone else. Grief is as real as great joy—and those who try to smother either can be a candidate for other problems, including illness.

Which brings me to still another point. When the shock begins to subside, you will be asked for what seems like the thousandth time, "How *are* you?" The question is often rhetorical, but when things quiet down, you might want to ask yourself the same question.

There is absolutely no doubt that strong emotions can have a direct and even sudden effect on matters of health. As soon as seems reasonable, make an appointment with your doctor for a general checkup. You may think you have no symptoms at all, except perhaps you are tired, are having difficulty sleeping, finding yourself depressed from time to time, and discovering that you have moments of anxiety. Nothing serious. These are symptoms, and even if your doctor offers no medication at all, if he only tells you that everything is in good working order, it will help your situation more than you can imagine. If, however, your physician finds that your emotional trauma might be giving you problems, the sooner you visit him or her, the better you will feel for the tasks ahead.

I believe that grief has a very definite purpose and that it should be encountered just like any other very serious event. I also believe that it has a beginning and an end.

We experience trauma in varying degrees all through life—little "deaths." The loss of a job after years of employment is a shock to the system and involves a series of situations that some may feel is worse than death—the loss of "face" and self-respect; the fear that others will look upon you as a failure, or worse, "all through." The loss is not only a matter of unemployment but also could include losing the family home or car, taking the youngsters out of college, or accepting a low-paying position in order to eat. Divorce is another form of death, when partnerships are dissolved, often with great bitterness. Again, children may be affected, and in some instances the process may create financial hardship on both sides. Still others might find severe trauma in moving to another city because of employment conditions, when the family must leave good friends of long standing, and when children must be taken out of a school in which they are happy and doing very well. Any of these situations may cause an emotional unbalance that cries out for logic.

But logic is hard to exercise when you find yourself off balance. Which brings us right back to counseling, no matter how informal. People come to me hoping for objectivity. I feel I can supply that because I am not enveloped in the same rapture they are. I see, but do not participate in, their fury. Often I can sight the solution quickly, other times I see a difficult, but not impossible, road ahead for them. And what is our method? Simple. We just talk it over.

What you are doing during your bereavement is meeting life's greatest test. It is a given that grief is about "losing." But there is another aspect: Grief is also for *growing*.

First of all, don't think you will feel better overnight or even in a few days. Your friends who have been through this before will tell you, "These things take time"—and that's true. Don't be in a hurry. Ride with the tide and let yourself relax as much as possible. When the "worst" is over, you may find things going along very smoothly. Then one day you may run into a friend on Main Street. That friend may ask, in all innocence, "And how's Charlie?" If it's the first such encounter, you may feel a little setback and become anxious about grieving all over again. But you won't. Trust me. You will convince yourself that grief is good and you've been through it; and while the question your friend asks may shake you just a bit, it's something you will have to answer over and over again. In time you will create a simple answer that will satisfy you and cover the situation handily.

I must tell you about Carrie, a woman now in her eighties who has the most terrific sense of humor of anyone I have ever known. She and her husband were as much in love as any couple I have ever met. When they entered a room together, it was as if a bright light had been turned on.

Cecil (she loved the name) ran a variety store in our village, and Carrie helped out in the evenings and was the store's window decorator. What she did to those windows on holidays was a joy to behold. Christmas was the Nativity—but she also liked the idea of having Santa Claus stuck in the chimney. Easter was lilies, but she also liked to display a cross-eyed Easter bunny sitting on top of a pile of eggs. Halloween drew kids from all over to see her ghosts float about the store—and she was very generous with the treats. The villagers said so many times,

"You can never tell when Cecil and Carrie are kidding."

Cecil was sorely missed when he died at age seventy. Carrie was lost for a while because it seemed that everything in the store bore Cecil's stamp—the little games, the jokes, the masks, the party favors. Cecil left behind his most valuable asset: his sense of humor. And Carrie carried on.

One afternoon some months after Cecil's death, a woman who had grown up in the village returned for a visit, stopped at the variety store for a box of candy, and was waited on by Carrie. After exchanging pleasantries, the woman asked, "How's Cecil these days?"

"Oh, he's having the time of his life," Carrie smiled. "He left me for someone else."

"Oh, I'm so sorry," the woman blurted.

"Oh, don't be sorry," Carrie said. "I'll catch up with him pretty soon now."

Carrie *will* catch up with Cecil, and I only wish I could attend the reunion. While Carrie often misses having Cecil around, she has gained a new reverence and love for life. She has found it with her daughter and son-in-law, in her grandchildren, and in Cecil's store.

Each time I think of this story, I have the feeling that Carrie never asked the question so many of us ask: "Why me?"

Why you? Why *me*? Priests have crises too. We watch our families and friends die, and we know we are mere mortals with human frailties and we'll die, too, when it's our time. If we have any advantage over a layperson, it may be that we have a better chance to get to know the whys so many people ask about and why they ask "Why?"

As your bereavement extends, you will come to learn that there is no satisfactory answer to the question, "Why?" One place to start is to realize and understand that we live in an imperfect world, and most of the imperfections are, to one degree or another, man-made. Some are aberrations of nature, so nature is not perfect either. We live in a world in which the only certainty is suffering. That is a cruel, hard fact. Benjamin Franklin's observation about death and taxes is on target with its simplicity. Whatever our religious persuasion might be, the message is the same: Experiencing a major loss is not optional.

Modern medicine has shown us that there are ways we can delay death. Smoking, for example, is accepted by the general public as a health hazard and a major cause of death in the world. Fifty years ago it was socially acceptable, and there was no thought about the dangers of secondhand smoke. The abuse of alcohol causes millions to die prematurely, as do any number of so-called recreational drugs. We can prolong our lives by eating sensibly, driving carefully, attending to small infections, getting a physical examination yearly, and looking both ways before we cross the street. In the overall picture, however, these precautions seem to be negated by our insistence in defiling our natural resources by polluting our rivers and lakes, and filling the air we breath with toxic fumes from our cars and manufacturing plants. But time has proven that with reasonable care we can lengthen our lifespan to some degree.

On the other hand, there are the innocents who never contribute an iota to their own illness or death, the "good people," young and old who are caught up in the circumstance of a disease that cannot yet be halted. Some die violently, the victims of another human's carelessness, stupidity, or disregard. Some are the targets of deranged minds, victims of killers. These are the ones for whom we weep the most. They did nothing, yet they have been deprived of life on earth.

Rather than ask "Why?" I suggest we ask "How?"

How shall we grieve?

That is the crux of the matter. It's not so important that we grieve, it's how we work through our grief.

Close friends have asked me, "Will my religion help me?"

That depends on what you mean by *religion*. Religion is a noun. A set of beliefs regarding the nature of the universe. What we really mean to ask is, "Will my *faith* give me hope?" And the answer to that is yes. Without faith there is no hope.

First you must realize there are some "givens." You *will* survive this loss. Although a loved one is dead, you will continue to live; therefore, you have a specific obligation to yourself. You may find it difficult to put yourself in the forefront at this juncture—particularly if you have been a caregiver to the deceased. Accept the simple fact that you are alive, and more than that, *you are still you.*

Your faith, based on your religious beliefs, can be of tremendous help when you are bereaved. For one thing, it will help you realize that death is temporary and *life* is permanent. Your faith will tell you that although the moment is sad in an earthly sense, it is not the end of anything. Your belief will not, in any way, diminish the pain you feel when someone you love dies. Your faith will not make the loss any less real, but it will comfort and sustain you and make it easier for you to recover from this period of grief. For some, grief is work and is a lengthy process; for those who are resilient, it is quickly over. But some will find that the load is heavy, that even little chores and simple duties seem overwhelming. Sometimes just remembering a telephone number is too much, and an ever-present cloud of silent sadness hovers everywhere.

However, there are some people who actually want the mourning process to continue indefinitely. I recall attending a party for members of the choir of one of our parishes and noticing a woman passing among the guests showing snapshots which seemed to be causing an uncomfortable undertone to the festivities. Her husband had been dead for over a year, yet she carried—and insisted on showing—pictures of him during their days together and during the last days of his illness in the nursing home. She was creating a social problem for herself by recounting the details of her husband's life and death to whomever she chanced to meet. In this case, her husband's death was probably the single most important thing that ever happened to her, and she seemed to want the kind words and sympathy that were heaped on her to continue. She probably will never understand why her friends began avoiding her, even though they loved her husband dearly and were saddened to see him die. It was almost impossible for that woman to leave that milestone behind and create a new and happy life.

Where does a person start? I might suggest starting with that often-quoted image we find in the Psalms: "Yea though I walk through the valley of the shadow of death, I will fear no evil, for thou art with me…"

It's been my experience that faith also helps overcome loneliness. It becomes your companion. It ties you to your religious community where you need not be alone. The church, the synagogue, or the mosque offer great supportive power and genuine friendship; and if idleness seems to be your nemesis, your place of worship will more than welcome volunteer services. You will always feel wanted there. If you simply want visitors, the church will happily oblige. There are more "shepherds" and caregivers out there than you might imagine. There are many ears open to listen.

As you become more able to cope with your loss, you will begin to realize by watching and listening to others that life, indeed, is not always fair, and everybody is subject to these realities. You will also be gratified to know that you will not be deserted in your circumstance. The only person who can get in the way of your recovery is you.

Having watched hundreds and hundreds of individuals deal with bereavement, I've often wished that we of the clergy somehow could create a magic potion or circumstance that would attack grief at the very outset and make it go away in an instant. We cannot do it. No drug will do it. Grief must run its course, but there is nothing to say the process can't be speeded up by your search for hope and holding on to your faith.

For various reasons, each of us would consider it a blessing if we could shorten our period of bereavement. A bereaved couple with growing children, for example, have a responsibility to allow the children's lives to go on, develop, and blossom. If the bereaved is an older person who finds the loss equally difficult to bear, we must make room to afford him or her solace and empathy. Looking after others will keep the bereaved going. Facing and fulfilling responsibility is part of the rehabilitation process, and it will make you feel wanted—and good.

12

THE QUALITY OF LIFE VS. DEATH

As people live longer, as the science of medicine becomes unbelievably more sophisticated, as "miracles" are performed daily in operating rooms all over the country, we find ourselves with a whole new set of decisions that didn't have to be made a half century ago. Old people died, as did accident victims, and those—young and old—with terminal conditions silently passed away.

Today we have support systems that do a miraculous job of prolonging life and keeping a patient alive long enough for a recovery process to set in. With this new capability, of course, comes a great deal of controversy. Who should decide how long to maintain life support? The patient? the family? the physician or society? Must each case be handled on an individual basis, or can generalized criteria be set up? If so, by whom? What factors must be taken into consideration regarding the quality of life of the patient or victim? What about family needs? What about expense?

A recent story from the New York courts received major media coverage. An elderly man had suffered through the long lingering illness of his wife, and at one point, he decided that as long as she was considered "brain dead," he would order the support systems stopped. The hospital officials and the doctors in charge did not agree with him or acknowledge his wish. His wife was kept on machines for some six weeks before she finally succumbed. The husband was promptly presented with a bill for over a hundred thousand dollars which, by now, he didn't have, his insurance and savings having been eaten up by his wife's long illness. He sold a few of his belongings in order to hire an attorney to take the matter to court. The case took longer than he thought and the attorney's fees mounted. Finally, a decision was handed down by a judge. The man, indeed, owed the hundred thousand-plus dollars, whether he disagreed with the hospital or not. As the case faded from importance in the media, it was learned that he could not afford an appeal and was about to lose his home—his last asset.

The ethical, the practical, and the spiritual elements of such a decision all converge here. The

ethical area concerns the obligation of the doctor
and other caregivers. The practical has to do with
how the family, the doctors, and the patient feel
about prolonging the life of a terminally ill patient
who has suffered great and unreasonable pain and
will, in all probability, die soon. The spiritual has to
do with one's religious beliefs, and often the family's
priest, rabbi, or minister becomes involved in the
decision making.

The questions plague everyone involved. "Are
we not playing God when we keep patients alive
only through the use of drugs or machines?" Or
"What do you say to patients who seriously request
the hospital staff to terminate their life because they
can no longer bear the despair or pain, or the pain
they see their family going through?"

My good friend and frequent associate, Rabbi
Marc Gellman, looks at a sixteenth century code of
Jewish law (Shulham Aruch) which says that a
dying person (gossess) is still like a living person in
all respects. Jewish law requires that nothing be
done to hasten death, to slow death down, or to
interfere with death. An analogy he cites is this: A
dying person is like a flickering candle near the end
of its burning. If you move it or touch it, it will go out.
Jewish law says we must carefully allow life to go out
on its own. If, for example, there is a wood chopper
outside the patient's window causing disturbing
sounds, which jar the patient into consciousness,
the wood chopper must be silenced.

There is, too, the story of Giuseppe Verdi, who, in 1901 at the age of eighty-seven, lay dying in his home in Milan. The great composer of *Rigoletto*, *Il Trovatore*, and *La Traviata*, was so revered in his adopted city that the townspeople spread thick layers of straw over the cobblestones in the street so that the noise from passing carts and wagons would not hasten his death.

There are in this and other countries various actions in favor of legalized euthanasia and "assisted suicides." Much media attention has been given to Michigan's "Doctor of Death," Jack Kevorkian, and the state's legislation that prohibited his helping terminally ill individuals commit suicide or, as the argument goes, assisting people in great pain to put themselves out of their own misery. In cases where the patient is not in control and on life-support systems, the decision to "pull the plug" is now often a court decision. Those opposed to anyone at all making these decisions look to hospice care and pain management. The modern arguments go something like this:

Pain generally has four different components: physical, psychological, social, and spiritual. Of these, physical pain is the most apparent as the cause of suffering. It is an alarm that indicates something is wrong with the body. Physical pain affects the whole person and can exceed its function as a warning signal. In the case of, say, an auto accident or extreme trauma, severe pain can drive a person to ask for removal of that pain at any price, even to the point of asking for death. This could also be the request of someone watching the patient suffer.

Then there is psychological pain that often comes with the thought of the inevitability of death, losing control, and letting go of hopes and dreams. Psychological pain takes on many ramifications because the thought process works as a trigger.

Social pain is caused by isolation and the reshaping of the conditions under which one suffers. There is the inability to communicate what one is experiencing, there is the embarrassment of having to be helped and cared for when the patient knows that the end is near. It is painful not to be able to be self-sufficient.

As a priest, I often see spiritual pain in a dying person. Mood swings will range from a loss of meaning and hope to quiet, even pleasant, anticipation of what is beyond. Everyone needs a certain framework for meaning—a reason to live and a reason to die. Biological facts of life take on new, urgent meanings. Has the patient led a good life? Is there anything that is still undone that must be done? Has this life been meaningful in any way? What will happen after death that he will miss? Will those she loves miss her? Will he ever see his loved ones again?

Physical pain is undoubtedly the easiest to control, but there is a feeling in some quarters that too much physical pain goes unrelieved. A Catholic document entitled *Care of the Dying,* published in

1993, suggests that as many as seventy-five percent of patients in pain are inadequately treated and sixty to ninety percent of those who are terminally ill experience moderate to severe pain—sufficient to impair physical functioning, mood, and social interaction. The document maintains that nearly twenty-five percent of cancer patients die in severe, unrelieved pain, the causes being that physicians are too timid in prescribing adequate medication or that a patient often chooses not to comply with a given therapeutic program to avoid side effects or because of the fear of losing control. Physical pain, then, is an important factor in looking at the implications of health care for the dying.

Extreme pain and misery in the terminally ill might be considered a reason to stop, or not to begin, medical treatment to prolong life. However, there is a history of decisions to do just that—decisions made by family members, attending physicians, and sometimes the patient. Active killing, even for mercy, is positively illegal in the United States, but cases involving the terminally ill and the cessation of treatment is a very cloudy area, and the courts have found that prosecution of physicians or family members in such cases is extremely difficult. Courts have ordered such things as transfusions, the return of a patient to respiratory machines, and other procedures, but generally only when the patient is a minor or a less than competent adult patient is involved. But there are still many district attorneys who would favor the prosecution of anyone who "pulls the plug" and allows even a terminally ill or brain-dead patient to die.

Facing a decision to allow death challenges us morally. It is the last kind of judgment we want to make, even with the advice and counsel of a doctor. However, modern medicine and its technical ability to prolong life during the most excruciating crises put this decision before doctors and families in increasing numbers.

An associate of mine in the Church, a former nun named Maureen, had experienced—along with her brothers—a long vigil as her mother lay dying. A family agreement had been made, with the mother very much a part of it, that when death was absolutely imminent and nothing could prevent it, and if the mother were on life support, that the support should be terminated. Clearly, my friend said, her mother had less than a day to live. Perhaps only a matter of hours. Because Maureen had been the bulwark of the family, the nun who had experienced dealing with the grief of others, the stolid nun whose strength had given her a keen understanding and a tremendous amount of compassion, she was named as the agent in this case. The brothers were afraid they couldn't handle it, so it would be up to the sister to sign the release the doctors needed.

"But," she said, "when I was handed the pen and looked at the paper, I was absolutely paralyzed. *I could not write my own name*. My fingers shook so that my brother had to take the pen from me. Although I had witnessed this phenomenon in others, we were certain that with my training and experience, I would be the last to succumb to a sudden surge of guilt. The simple task became a problem of immense magnitude. As much as the doctors and my brothers reassured me, I was helpless in this emotional trap. My brothers signed the paper.

"I had arrived home only a few hours before my mother passed away. When my brother called, he said, 'Maureen, removing the support wouldn't have mattered either way. It was time for Mother to go—and she went peacefully and painlessly.' That made things easier. When I got over the initial shock—for regardless of how long the patient lingers, there is a shock in knowing of the finality—I realized that this was a rather common reaction that people have when they feel they may be intervening in the termination of life. But I would add, too, that when practicality sets in, you realize that what you have done is something for which you should feel absolutely no guilt. No more guilt than, say, arranging for the burial. But, whatever my experience, there will be many who find the task both haunting and daunting. For many reasons."

Certainly the ability to sustain life is not bad. There are thousands, perhaps millions, of people who are alive and active today because of the miracles of modern medicine. The debate comes in the way the power over life and death is used. What one individual might see as a gift of life, another might see as a living death. If a patient's prognosis is that machine-driven resuscitators would still render a patient bedridden, ventilator-dependent, and unable to communicate with anyone ever, should that person be allowed to die?

All states recognize to one degree or another that the patient's desires be considered. Living wills and powers of attorney in medical cases have some status in every state, although that status is not the same everywhere. The situations vary with state legislators. Many states limit the kinds of life-support treatment that can be stopped or not started even when a living will is present. Some states narrow the restrictions to such procedures as artificial nutrition and hydration. In the complexities of laws among states, even certain kinds of medication are involved in court decisions.

The amount of attention the media has focused on court cases involving living wills has caused millions of Americans to consider making one. Proponents suggest that anyone who wants to avoid life-sustaining medical treatment in circumstances where the individual would be put through a cruelly agonizing remainder of his or her life, where life would continue only in a coma, or where a brain-dead situation would cause undue hardship emotionally and financially on the family, that person should arrange for a living will. Telling your loved ones what you want if such a situation should occur can lift a great burden in decision making. While a living will might have some limitations in what the law will allow, a great deal of uncertainty can be avoided by leaving such a document. What those familiar with living wills suggest is that you set up a "health-care power of attorney."

The problem with the family making such a decision is that if even one member disagrees with the procedure either way, physicians may be afraid to act, anticipating consequences that could be unpleasant if not threatening to their very practice of medicine.

There are several things to consider should you desire to create a living will, the first of which is to find out about the laws in your state. This generally can be answered by your family lawyer or, if you do not retain one, by your family doctor. If your doctor is noncommittal or doesn't know, ask where you can get such information. Your local state legislator can certainly answer the question for you as a service to a constituent. There are organizations that have such information ready for you, notably the American Association for Retired Persons which now has branches and consultants in nearly every major community in the nation. Other organizations that may help you are those devoted to education regarding serious illnesses such as AIDS, cancer, diabetes, kidney and lung disease.

Typical requirements are quite simple for a living will. You state your intentions, have the document dated, witnessed, signed, and notarized. There are a few books in your public library that are devoted to the making of living wills, so you might want to start there. The advantage of using a printed "primer" is that it will cover many issues involved in creating such a document and you may want to study it before signing a state form, drafting your own living will, or having it drafted by an attorney.

Extremely important is your selection of someone who would act as your agent or your health-care power of attorney. This particular agent would not necessarily be the person who has your complete power of attorney over all matters, financial and otherwise, but would be involved only in any health-care situation where you would be unable to make important decisions for yourself. In selecting some-one to represent you, be sure it is someone who knows you well, knows your health history, understands your wishes completely, and above all, is absolutely trustworthy, because you are assigning a life and death decision-maker, and the life is yours. Your agent should be someone you perceive as one who is capable of making painful decisions under great stress, someone who would be able to push for action should a decision be necessary.

Most states have set up certain requirements for the acknowledgment of a living will. It's generally required that the patient be an adult, nonpregnant, competent, or afflicted with a condition in which death is imminent. All fifty states and the District of

Columbia have "forms of declaration" available; however, they vary in content, intent, and length and some contain certain choices a prospective patient must make. In all states, your document, including any pages you may add, must be witnessed and notarized. It would be wise to obtain your state's form and go over it with an attorney or someone familiar with legalese to determine what the form allows or doesn't allow.

Arkansas has the shortest and simplest. It reads:

> If I should have an incurable or irreversible condition that will cause my death within a relatively short time, or, if I should become permanently unconscious, and I am no longer able to make decisions regarding my medical treatment, I direct my attending physician, pursuant to the Arkansas Rights of the Terminally Ill or Permanently Unconscious Act, to withhold or withdraw treatment that only prolongs the process of dying and is not necessary to my comfort or to alleviate pain and to follow the instructions of _____ whom I appoint as my Health Care Proxy to decide whether life-sustaining treatment should be withheld or withdrawn.

Then follow places for signatures of the prospective patient and witnesses, along with

addresses and telephone numbers. It's that simple in
Arkansas, but in other states, such as California,
New Hampshire, and Nevada, the forms are much
longer and more complicated.

In making additions to such a form, you may
want to include special instructions due to a
preexisting health condition that should be taken
into consideration should you not be able to
communicate. So it would be wise to ask for counsel
to be certain your living will is clear and specific, and
does what you want it to do. I would also suggest that
you update your living will every few years, taking
into consideration any changes in your health.

If, on the other hand, you might be the one to
execute the wishes of the matter of a living will, it is
important that you don't feel all alone in making
your decision, or you may find a harrowing shadow
following you: the notion that perhaps you may have
made the wrong decision. The issues you would be
confronting are not only legal but also physical and
emotional. You will want to talk with someone who
has been there before, certainly the doctor or doctors
involved, and your lawyer, if you have one.
Remember, too, that you not only have a legal
question but also a spiritual one, so you should
consider your priest, minister, or rabbi as an intimate
friend, and discuss not only what you *can* do, but
what you *ought* to do.

If you are asked to be the agent of a loved one
who has made a living will, it would be wise to take

some time—long before it's necessary, if indeed it ever *is* necessary—to discuss such things as organ donations, whether the will calls for burial or cremation, and other practical matters. You may consider them indelicate subjects early on, but the more that can be settled in your own mind should the need ever arise, the stronger you will be should you ever have to face the situation. In the final analysis, after soliciting as much input as you can from those you trust, you should be certain the decision is your own and that you can live with it.

If you have a living will, or are an agent in a living will, it's likely you already have a regular will, and that it's in a safe place where someone you trust will know where to find it if anything should happen to you. If you haven't gone through the simple process of making a will, or having an attorney make one for you, I cannot stress enough how important it is to have one. If you have ever considered what your wishes would be should you be taken out of the picture, a will is necessary, otherwise it may be the role of the state in which you live to divide your assets in any way the law sees fit. Dying intestate can not only cause your family undue hardship and possible financial crises due to the expense of taking claims to court, but the emotional stress and family disagreements that may ensue can be unduly hard on your chosen heirs. A simple will will do, and the cost of having an attorney draw up a standard will is minimal.

There are a few other things that everyone should take care of long before the prospect of death is even considered. I call it "inventory." These are little details that many people often put off until it's too late.

Your closest trusted family member or friend, or both, should have access to a list of where "everything" is should anything happen to you. You may not realize how complicated and involved your financial and personal life has become. Over and above having a will you should list:

All insurance policies. The name of the companies, policy numbers, premium amounts, deductible benefits, your agent's name and telephone number. Include not only life insurance, but insurance policies on your home, car, boat, jewelry, or anything else on which a policy has been written.

Savings and investments. Names, addresses, and phone numbers of your brokers and banks or financial institutions holding your stocks, bonds, funds, or cash. List all accounts by number, including passbooks and checking.

Safe deposit box contents. Make a key available to someone you trust or leave instructions on where the key can be found. Without the key, your spouse, family member, or other survivor may need a court order to venture into this bank-controlled mine of information. If there are papers that are extremely valuable to you, such as the deed to your home or the title to your car, receipts for expensive items, birth certificates, military discharge papers, or simple papers to which you can refer, make copies for your home file.

Current financial standing. It would be wise to keep a running record of all your assets, liquid or otherwise, such as cash on hand, savings and checking account balances, size of your mortgage, lines of credit and at what institutions, credit balances on major purchases, credit-card debt, if any, property taxes, real estate value of your home, and any other items that require constant attention. This may sound like "playing banker," but should an emergency arise, a list of this sort could prove invaluable not only for someone who would be in charge of handling your affairs but for tax purposes as well. No tax offices are sympathetic or even sensitive to the human condition.

While death and taxes are certain, death has no timetable that any human can find reliable. The people you leave when you depart this earth will find the pain of bereavement straining the emotions enough. Whatever can be done by planning in advance will ease the burden just that much more.

13

LIFE AFTER DEATH

The very thought of life after death is awesome, to say the least. To accept Christian theology may be difficult for some people because it taxes the imagination. The presence of a soul, the idea of Heaven and Hell, the ability to understand that a spiritual "beyond" exists, that reaching that place is practically instantaneous—all this may seem incomprehensible. But then, if we look back over the accomplishments of humankind in the last two hundred years, things might come into perspective and be a little easier to understand.

Two hundred years is the blink of an eye in the history of the world. Consider a declaration that might have been made in the mid-1700s. Let's say that a man of great respect, an erudite teacher, makes some predictions. He claims that soon we will no longer write with quill and ink, but on a machine that will print our thoughts as fast as we can move our fingers, and transmit them to anywhere in the world at the rate of 136 thousand miles per second. He claims that a person will be able to speak into a machine in New York, or anywhere, and be heard all over the world, and even more astonishing, will be seen in a moving, color picture. He claims that man will fly like a bird in machines that will be bigger than three log cabins, carrying hundreds of people through the air at the rate faster than three hundred fifty miles an hour, thirty miles a second; that we will be able to cross the ocean in a matter of hours, that a man will stand on the *moon* and will be able to talk to us on earth as though we were in the next room. This eighteenth century oracle declares that smallpox, polio, and diphtheria will be wiped out with vaccines. And probably most astonishing of all is his notion that candles will no longer be used for lighting a home, that all we will have to do is push a switch on the wall and cold bright light will illuminate the room as if there were a thousand candles. That man in the mid-1700s would be considered insane, dangerous, and probably a heretic.

But when we consider what human beings have accomplished in so short a time, we must also consider this: No human invented the maple seed that falls from the tree in the autumn propelled by an aerodynamically perfect single wing. No one invented the lungs, the kidneys, the heart, or the brain; and no parent had the power or privilege of designing his or her own offspring. No animal designed its own protective coloring. No human created the great rivers or oceans, the mountains or the deserts. No human created electricity. No human set in motion the order of the natural world. The universe itself is awesome beyond compare—and we had nothing to do with it. There is a greater Power than ours, and it has been articulated millions of times by millions of people who recognize it. While I agree that it is difficult to envision the wonders of God in practical terms, these wonders are real and do exist.

The world's greatest human minds have been deliberating these phenomena for centuries. Albert Einstein, in contemplating his own works, said that his own theory of relativity was only a sort of "suggestion." That tackling the equation of the universe was like a termite attacking the Empire State Building. Dr. Einstein put it this way in a paper he wrote in 1930 titled *What I Believe*:

> To know what is impenetrable to us really exists, manifesting itself as the highest wisdom and the most radiant beauty, which our dull faculties can comprehend only in the most primitive forms—this knowledge, this feeling, is at the center of true religiousness. In this sense only, I belong to the ranks of truly religious men.

We learn about life after death from Jesus, Himself. In John 11:25-26, we read: "Jesus told her, 'I am the resurrection and the life. Those who believe in me, even though they die, will live, and everyone who lives and believes in me will never die.'"

Or take John 6:51: "I am the living bread that came down from heaven. Whoever eats of this bread will live forever."

The Scriptures are filled with these promises, and they are not uttered idly.

Part of our fear of dying is that we *know* what's in this world, but we are not sure of what's in the next. You may say to yourself, *This world allows me to do certain things, to see and hold my grandchildren, to work at my job, to enjoy my friends. I will miss this world.* Or you may grieve when you think of a dying son or daughter whose potential will never be fulfilled. Of course, there is sorrow in these situations. I often hear, "Why did he have to die now? He cared for so many people."

From reading the research of the world's most respected experts in the matter of death, and talking with hundreds of people as they were dying, I've come to believe that we *are* transported to God, and that life does not end when we die—that it takes on a new and full meaning. That dying is as easy as going from one room to the next.

When we have traveled to God, we will be greeted by friends and relatives and significant people in our lives, and these will be the people who will bring us into the presence of God. What do I think it's like to meet God? I sincerely believe that it will be the most loving, most peaceful, most exhilarating, wonderful experience that we will ever have.

I see the person of Jesus walking among us, very much as He did in this world, healing, helping, teaching, bringing people together. I believe that people who have died are still connected to us. They have another reality that they're dealing with now. They have a new world, but they are still connected with us, and when we die, we will actually meet them and interact with them. Our family in this world will be our family in the next world—only it will be a little bigger.

So I believe that when people die, life doesn't end. It takes on a new and fuller meaning, and the best way to connect with those who have gone ahead is to pray for them. When I celebrate a Mass, I often offer that Mass for some individual who is either still here with us or who has gone to Heaven. It is the most beautiful gift I can give.

I believe there are "levels" of life after death. Christians call these Heaven, Purgatory, and Hell. Heaven is the sanctified state. Purgatory is a place to make up for sins. Hell is a place where there is no hope. I believe that each of us is going to find, with God, the place where we deserve to be. We will see ourselves more clearly than ever—even see ourselves for the first time. We will realize that we have done some things in a virtuous way, and we will know what things we have done that are evil. I believe that God will let us experience what we've done to others.

I believe that God will ask us to do something special in the next world. The talents God gave us to use in this world will be enhanced in the next. The work that made us the happiest here will continue to make us happy. I believe that God will magnify the deepest values in our lives.

I sometimes think of a very devout woman who is one of the kindest people I know. As an organist, violinist, and choir director, she has devoted her life to the music of God. Her simplest wish is that in the next world, the Lord will assign her a harp. I believe she'll get her harp.

I think it's not just happenstance that I'm a priest, and I believe that I will have a calling even in the next world because I will discover those who will need someone with whom to reflect, who will have questions about the next life.

I'm often asked very pragmatic questions about life after death. A mother, in tears, at her son's funeral said, "My boy was addicted, Father. As you know, he died of an overdose. Will I see him in Heaven?"

I told her that I believed when her son goes into the light of God, he won't be rejected, but will become aware of his own deficiencies. Many things will be lifted from his eyes, and he will know he'll be healed, and that allowing himself to die the way he did was not the right thing to do. He will have the help of God. It's never God's intent to destroy anyone. It's never God's intent to keep anybody from the light. That's why he sent Jesus to us. He wanted us to see that He loved us enough to send His own son—who died for us.

Is there a Hell? I believe there is. The question, of course, is—what kind of people are there? I think in Hell one would find people who never loved, never wanted love, and never cared about love. There are people in this world who make big mistakes. Usually those mistakes are not characteristic of their lives. But if those big mistakes were totally symbolic of who the person was, and symbolic of that person who, even in the presence of the light of God, would choose to live a loveless sinful life, then that individual would choose Hell.

But I believe that children who found no joy on earth will find great joy in Heaven. The down-trodden, abused, put-upon, and beaten individuals who fell into earthly traps of evil through no fault of their own, will find peace, solace, and happiness in Heaven.

A few years ago, I had the good fortune of being able to work with Mother Teresa, and while I was with this saintly woman, I became aware of some of my own deficiencies—things I wanted to correct. Mother Teresa is the personification of a woman who *lives* in the light of God on earth. Simply being with her, I wanted, more than ever, to go out and do good things with my life. She represents what the Church is saying about the Kingdom of God. It begins now, but will be fulfilled later on. She sets an example and shows us that if only we can grow in the love of God here, and if we can see that we really are each other's caretakers, if only we can live in this spirit, it will bring us to know what the next world is all about.

In Heaven, inspired by the peacefulness and the wonder of the light of God, we're going to see where we belong. We will all want to improve. I believe that God allowed me to meet Mother Teresa in order to feel what it must be like to meet God. In meeting the warmth and reality of God, we will see the good and the bad, and we will see what we have done wrong, and we will know how to improve upon it.

What about those who feel they've found happiness and success on earth? These people die too. A fifty-eight-year-old friend of mine told me, "I was really good in business. I made a lot of money. I've given my family every earthly thing they could want or need. I was a killer in industry. My family loved me. We did exciting, loving things together. It never entered my mind that I would die at this age. I don't know how to deal with this. I'm used to being in control, and now the expectations I had in life won't be fulfilled."

My answer was, "Dying simply means an

adjustment to the expectations we had in life. You will be fulfilled in the next life."

Is it easy to die? Of course not, but considering that we will be greeted by our loved ones, friends, and God, and live day in and day out doing good things with one another, sharing our talents, meeting new people, learning new languages, moving beyond illness and disease, replacing tears with laughter, it's difficult to imagine why anyone wouldn't feel comfortable knowing that God will bring us and our friends home some day.

There are those who contend they have already had a glimpse of what lies beyond. One Sunday I was greeted by a man named Roger who seemed very ebullient. For a man who had only recently been released from the hospital after a serious operation, he was full of fervor. After the usual inquiry into the state of his health, I noted that he seemed to be extremely happy about something. "Father Tom," he said, "I had a near-death experience. During my operation, I nearly died. I was lifted out of my body and brought into the presence of the most wonderful, warm, peaceful light I've ever experienced. I saw colors I never saw before. I met God. The presence in the light was God. He was so warm and accepting. I saw my relatives. I reached out for my dad. I felt a very strong connection. I've never felt a love like this before. The only reason I knew that I hadn't died was that my arms went right through my dad. Then I felt myself coming back.

"As the reality of my situation returned, I realized that I had been wondering all my life why I was here. The question would cross my mind, then I'd get busy and forget about it for a while. But all through my lifetime, it kept popping up. 'Why am I here?' But in that moment, God showed me why I'm here. Life is much simpler than I thought it was. It's just a question of how to love and to care and to reach out. In those few moments I learned how to love and how to be loved in return."

"Are you all right now?" I asked him.

"Well, they couldn't get all the cancer, and I know I have only a short time, Father, but I can tell from what I've seen that I have absolutely nothing to fear." Since that morning I have heard from many people who claim to have had a glimpse into the beyond. All descriptions were very positive. They all talked about that light and the kind of peace that only God can bring.

Twenty years ago, when psychiatrist Raymond Moody began to publish his research on near-death experiences, he was a pioneer in a field that was viewed as merely an academic curiosity. Now he is one of the senior figures in a growing field of researchers and popular authors who have introduced reams of research based on personal accounts of people who seemed to have "pierced the veil" between now and the hereafter, and come back to tell about it.

Critics have called these studies everything

from promises of an afterlife, to medical idiosyncrasies, to delusions of the devil, to dreams under the influence of anesthesia, to the whims of publicity-seekers. Some critics dismiss the studies; others, including prominent theologians, are taking an interested look. The research is so copious that it's difficult to ignore it any longer.

Pollster George Gallup, Jr., for instance, estimated in his 1982 book, *Adventures in Immortality*, that about eight million people in the United States at that time had some kind of near-death encounter which they were willing to talk about.

A cardiologist at Emory University Medical Center in Atlanta interviewed all his patients who were resuscitated from heart attacks in the mid 1980s. About a third reported having a near-death experience. If these reports show nothing else, they indicate that these experiences have had a profound effect on the people involved.

While near-death experiences are intriguing, most Catholic theologians do not view them as proof-positive of an afterlife, but no one has yet been able to say definitely why and how a near-death experience occurs.

The best-selling book on the subject is *Life After Life*, by Dr. Raymond Moody. He cites his study as an "investigation into the remarkable similarity to experience among those who have 'returned from the end of this life.'" The conclusions are left to the reader, but Dr. Moody presents an unemotional analysis which, he says, calls for a continuing study of the life-ending phenomena. Dr. Elisabeth Kübler-Ross, in her introduction to Dr. Moody's book, admits that Dr. Moody should be prepared for criticism, mainly from members of the clergy and those individuals who consider the subject taboo.

A typical story among the one hundred fifty case studies Dr. Moody investigated has a person dying, hearing himself pronounced dead by the doctor. The person then feels himself moving very rapidly through a tunnel—either bright or dark—and then suddenly sees his own body from a distance. He watches the doctors try to resuscitate him and notices that he still has a body, but one of a very different sort with different "powers." Then things begin to happen. Others come to meet and help him. He sees the spirits of relatives and friends, and then he senses a warm, bright light. Someone asks him some questions, nonverbally, about his life, and helps him along. He sees a panoramic playback of the major events of his life. But now he is approaching a barrier which is the limit between earthly life and this new life. Despite the warmth of the situation, he realizes that his time has not yet come, and he must go back. He does not want to return because he is overwhelmed by the intense feelings of joy, love, and peace. Despite his feelings, he somehow reunites with his earthly body and lives.

Most subjects try to tell others about these experiences, Dr. Moody says, but they have trouble doing so. First of all, they cannot find adequate words. They find that people tend to scoff, so eventually they stop talking about it. Still, the experience affects their lives deeply, especially their views about death and its relationship to life.

The individual details of these accounts vary somewhat, but what seems to have impressed Dr. Moody is that basically the events are very similar. Most talked about a dark tunnel or valley and then a bright, warm light. Many report an out-of-body experience in which they become spectators to their own near-death. Far and away the majority of Dr. Moody's subjects reported that they did find themselves in another body upon release from the "physical" one.

Dr. Bruce Greyson, a professor of psychiatry at the University of Connecticut Medical School, has spent twenty years studying people who have had near-death experiences. He notes that because curiosity about the subject crosses professional, denominational, and cultural lines, there is a persistent public appetite for scientific research and personal accounts of near-death experiences. So I expect we will be seeing many more studies on this very-difficult-to-prove phenomenon. Dr. Moody says he is not a "religious" person, but believes that his work has shown that God is love, and that the most important thing we can do while we are alive is to learn how to love.

That conclusion squares with my belief about

our lives after death. It just happens to be that my own conclusions are based on a different set of circumstances. Without doubt, there will be many attempts to explain these near-death episodes. Some will set forth the idea that they are part of the supernatural experience. Others will find scientific explanations that are physiological as well as neurological, which result in hallucinations and delusions. But fad or otherwise, I find one constant that pleases me...

God is love. God is there. God is waiting for us. We will be happy and at peace.

14

TO LIVE AGAIN

We began with death and we will end with life. This is the denouement of working one's way through the treacherous terrain of grief. Grief begins with a painful loss, but it could mean the beginning of a new life. Not that you have forgotten your loss. You never will, and you will often think of the one you have lost. But having worked through grief, you will find that you have developed a new strength of character. You will find within yourself strength you never imagined you had. Sometimes it takes a major event to bring out those strengths. This, of course, doesn't give you immunity from future loss, but it will help you greatly to cope with and understand anything that might come your way.

As time goes by, you will discover that you can regain a full life after experiencing a death. It takes work, and you must allow time to help ease yourself into a new lifestyle. Many people can help you if only you let them, especially those people who have suffered similar losses.

The first two or three months after the death of a loved one are the most difficult. By now all vestiges of shock and numbness are gone and the full impact of what has happened is upon you. You have been through the agony of filling out and filing insurance claims, death certificates, and Social Security forms. You've become annoyed at a bureaucratic system that refuses to believe anyone has died without substantial proof, placing the burden of proof on the survivor. The details never seem to stop.

A friend of mine lost her husband very suddenly and was swept up in a flurry of paperwork that was extraordinarily tedious and confusing to her. Even with a valid will, she still had problems with the banks, with two insurance companies, with the people who held her husband's mutual fund and stock accounts. She actually ran out of cash trying to collect her own money. "There were so many things to remember," she said, "so many things to think about that I actually forgot to change the greeting on my telephone answering machine. Finally, a friend of mine told me that she called the house and heard, 'Hello, this is Tom. Neither Barbara nor I are here right now...'"

The danger of that three-month period is that the cruel real world demands your time and your attention. Business offices don't send sympathy cards; they still send bills and expect them to be paid. The IRS will not send flowers; they will be right on tap to tell you what your tax situation is. You will look at the goings-on around you and say to yourself, *Doesn't anybody care? Doesn't anybody know what I'm going through?*

More than once I have had a survivor come to me during this period and confess to having entertained the idea of suicide. Self-destructive thoughts are not unusual, but I treat them very seriously even though I know the chances of a bereaved person doing something so foolish are practically nil.

If you are having real difficulties in handling the death of a loved one, and your friends are concerned about you, try to find a support group. As I suggested earlier, your own church or synagogue is a good place to start. If you feel you need serious counseling, a pastoral caregiver will be extremely supportive, I'm sure.

Although it's seldom mentioned, hospital and insurance surveys have shown that a few months after a major loss, you could be quite vulnerable to the onset of serious illness. You have probably heard that when a spouse dies, the surviving widow or widower lives only a year or so longer. It happens frequently enough to give it more than a passing thought. Very reliable medical surveys indicate that within a year after the loss of a spouse or close relative, twenty-five percent of the survivors underwent a diminishing of their natural immune system. The symptoms are often described as "mysterious." Patients complain of a high fever, chronic headache pain, exhaustion, and weakness. The survivor may consider these symptoms to be "psychosomatic." Most doctors will tell you that few true symptoms are psychosomatic.

Care for yourself by getting a thorough checkup. Make a list of any physical problems, including rapid heart rate, weight loss, pains anywhere in the body, dizziness or anything you feel is not quite "right."

Realize what you've been through and make plans to give yourself a well-deserved break. You have been through the same stages of dying as your beloved. You must work at reaching the stage of true acceptance.

Start looking at the calendar again, this time with an eye to making plans for holidays, reunions, visits, and vacations you've been putting off or ignoring. Even if the death of a spouse, for instance, didn't leave you in good financial order, there are things you can do and places you can go that will lighten your heart. If you are left "well-fixed," don't feel guilty about spending a little money on yourself. If you had always wanted to visit London or Paris or Rome, find a companion and treat yourself to a new experience. It's not being selfish, it's a matter of therapy.

You probably noticed at the outset of your

bereavement that your priorities in life had changed radically. You realized, as you never had before, what was really important and what was trivial, which problems needed immediate attention and which could wait. You couldn't be bothered worrying about who thought well of you and who didn't—who said unkind things and who didn't. If you had written down a list of day-to-day priorities before the death of your spouse or kin, and wrote a similar list today, the lists would probably be quite different.

Have you ever wished you could really get your priorities in order and not let "little things" bother you? Well, now is the perfect opportunity. Give yourself permission to enjoy the rest of your life in the best way you know how. You may think it trite and old-fashioned to rationalize that he or she "would have wanted it that way," but that rationalization is probably right on the mark.

In time you will encounter the first anniversary of the death of the person you cared for so much. You will feel you must mark that day, and if you're so inclined, it would be a good idea. The anniversary date of a great loss needn't be marked on your calendar. Every widow or widower can tell you the date and even the hour of the loss of a husband or wife. The anniversary of the death of a loved one is significant. It will bring a mixture of sadness and hope. You will be reminded of the days you first knew each other, of the pleasant times you had together, and you will recall your trials as well as your victories.

The first anniversary may carry a little of that old anger you had when things looked the blackest for you, but you will find it vanishing a little more easily than it had in the months before. You will discover that you are feeling a little less sorry for yourself now than you did a year ago.

Plan that day. It's an important day. If you work, take the day off if you can. Start the day in your church. It's a wonderful place to remember and commune with your loved one. There is something about starting this day in a way that will make you feel stronger and better. It's an appropriate time to go to church, and it certainly is an appropriate reason.

You may want to drop a few notes to those close to you who were especially helpful during your early bereavement. They don't have to be long or emotional, or even mention the anniversary, just a few notes to say thanks for being your friend. I received such a note from a woman whom I had counseled during the time her husband was near death. I was so impressed with the simplicity of what she said that I thought I would pay her a visit on the first anniversary of her loss. I telephoned first and was told to stop by anytime. At noon, I found her hard at work in her garden.

"Hi, Father," she said. "I looked for you in church this morning, but I must have missed you."

"I can't be there every minute or I wouldn't be able to take time out to visit good friends," I said.

"Your garden is doing beautifully, considering the weather."

"Well, John was the gardener. He was the putterer. And he loved these plants. I was going to sell the tools or give them away, but then I thought if John loved the garden that much, maybe there was something I was missing. And there was. I'm not as good as John was, but I'd really miss these flowers."

There, I thought, was the perfect antidote for a year of bereavement.

Other suggestions for a first anniversary might be a dinner date with a good friend who knows about your loss and how you feel.

It would be an excellent time to make new plans for the next year, to set some new goals for yourself. You might even consider going back to school, taking some courses that would either enhance your aspirations or be plain fun.

Do not struggle with the sense of being disloyal to a deceased spouse.

As you pass the one-year milestone, you will most likely find that you are having more "good" days than bad ones, that nighttime doesn't bother you as much as it used to, that it's easier to laugh again, that you will be able to watch a movie and let yourself be totally engrossed in the story.

Once you have passed the second anniversary of your loss, your primary focus will be on adapting to the new life you have created for yourself.

These time periods are arbitrary, based very

much on my own observations and discussions with persons in the medical and psychiatric communities and surveys I have studied to enhance my work in the psychological area of my calling. If you should find your time of bereavement shorter or longer, that's fine. There is no fixed clinical schedule of recovery from a loss. Bereavement is not an exact study. We know almost to the day the time it takes for conception to delivery of a human baby, but we have no way of telling when grief will subside and a new life will begin. Some people grieve forever. The lucky ones are able to build on their ability to accept what is inevitable.

If you are a surviving spouse, the idea of remarriage might occur to you. I have been asked many times how long the period of mourning should be before one considers a new husband or wife. That, of course, depends on so many factors that no serious advice can be given on the matter. One year? two years? four months? What was the relationship between the couple before the death of the spouse? Are there financial considerations? Is it true love or mere loneliness? Add any number of additional questions. It's entirely up to you, your conscience, and your God.

From time to time you will look back over the recent past and be rather self-conscious of your grieving period. Grief doesn't require anyone's permission, just yours; and it's very important that you give yourself that permission.

Immediately after your loss you probably found yourself tossing and turning at night, eating meals at odd times, or skipping meals altogether. You would find yourself slipping into a reverie and picturing old moments and hours of the past; but as time went along, you began to adopt a new regimen. You may have established a rather new set of manners and mores. You are eating breakfast at a certain time, lunch is rather regular, and while the dinner hour is much different now, you are becoming accustomed to it. This is good because it means you are settling into a comfortable pattern, although it may be a completely different pattern than you followed before your loss.

Someplace in the back of your mind you will hear, for a long time, a little voice asking, *I wonder what he would have thought of this* or *I wonder if she would approve of that?* That point of reference will do no harm unless you let it lead to indecision or confusion. But the choices are now yours and you are the head of the committee. You must be able to say, "*I* like that" or "*I* want to do that." The decisions will be many, as they always were—furniture, the color of the kitchen, the newspapers you subscribe to, the place you do your banking, even the place you shop for groceries and the things you choose to eat.

A psychologist friend of mine who writes a local newspaper column is full of ideas on the subject, having suffered a severe loss herself and recovering quite nicely. She found herself feeling a little guilty about being especially kind to herself when her husband wasn't there to enjoy things with her. When this wave would hit her, she busied herself with what she called "dirty work." She cleaned the toilets, scrubbed the hall floor, drained the rusty water from the furnace and replaced it with fresh water. She washed her white things and hung them on the line to dry instead of stuffing them in the dryer. She peeled carrots and potatoes and made herself a stew. By then, she said, she felt she had "earned" a little self-compassion. "I learned in my studies that I can allay anxiety by literally throwing myself into work I hate to do. I know that may not be for everybody, but it's worth a try."

Some people will still bother you. It's part of the law of life that just when you think things are going swimmingly, somebody comes along and throws you a curve that sends you reeling. It may be even a slight, unconsciously uttered, unfortunate remark. Or it might be a head-on biting criticism, something you feel you should have replied to, but didn't. You must not let little things "haunt" you. Easier said than done, because at almost any stage of bereavement—early or late—you are quite vulnerable. Years ago they called it being "touchy." You must consciously build up a resistance to "touchiness" with the same vigor that you would use to build up your physical well-being. Doing otherwise could conceivably start a process of withdrawal. This could undo months of healthy rearrangement of your life.

As you proceed with your rearranged life, you may find a friend or relative who is now going through what you experienced. Your first thought will probably be, *Oh, no! I **know** what they're going through. I don't know how I can handle this.*

However, I believe there is a marvelous mystery about grief. The more you share the grief of others, the more in charge of your own grief you will be. Stories of suffering servicemen in wartime often tell of the strength and comfort one wounded serviceman would give another. A soldier or sailor could easily give emotional sustenance to someone who had suffered the same hardship. When you share your struggles with others and listen to their stories, you will realize that the pain you suffered gives you a special insight and an ability to help another individual only because you really understand his or her dilemma. You can be of extra special comfort to them—and yourself.

There is one other thing to check on as you work your way through bereavement: your self-esteem. Ask yourself quite bluntly, and aloud, in front of a mirror: "How am I feeling about myself today?" Your answer can be anything from "I'm going out there and knock 'em dead!" to "I want to crawl back into bed and shut out the whole world." The latter, of course, is the last thing you want to hear yourself say. But, you don't have to want to "knock 'em dead," either. If you simply feel pretty good, that's good enough. It's a good way to start the day and indicates that things are going to get better.

It's vital that you like yourself. At some point you simply must forgive yourself for anything and everything you may have done or felt that you might consider "wrong," whether real or imagined. You don't have to set up a self-confessional, nor do you have to articulate anything. If you have caused any hurt that can be corrected, make a note to correct it—then do it and forget. It might seem like an odd exercise, but you should keep telling yourself that you are you, and you are good, and you are kind, and you are needed, and you can help others. If you can really convince yourself of this, you have won the battle. Once you are sure you are your own person, you will find that you truly *are* good and you truly *are* needed and will almost automatically receive the respect you deserve. If your hurt is slow in going away, you may have to do this exercise more than a few times, but do it.

In your new life, you'll have an exceptional number of choices—choices you may not have had before. It's not that your choices were limited when your loved one was alive—just that you had a different set of choices.

It will be good for you to keep busy doing the things you like to do—things that are fun for you. And you can experiment.

If you are in business and your company has a position that would require a move to a part of the country you might find enjoyable, you might want to consider it now.

If you've always had a yen to be an actor but never had the time to find out how good you'd be, contact a community theater group and try out for a play or musical. If you don't make it, but still love the kind of people who love the theater, offer your service as a stagehand, a painter, a costume designer, a ticket taker—and see how suddenly your services will be required. And as ye paint, so shall ye learn how to perform.

If you've always wanted to write, take a night-school writing course in, say, popular fiction. Then —write. Don't worry about not selling your first novel to the movies; the very task of putting words on paper could make you happy. Or, when you write, write to or *for* someone and send the manuscript to that person. You'll be amazed at how soon your friend will realize your writing ability.

If painting for fun or profit ever crossed your mind, buy an easel and some paints, and just start. Who should care about what you paint? Only you.

There are hundreds of directions in which you can go in search of busy things that will fill your days and evenings; but if you already work and like what you do, this might be a good time to think about what you can do better, how you might be more innovative in your career and move yourself up in your profession. If you are a designer, work out new ideas at home. If you are a typist, find out how you can make it to the next grade.

Success is no sin.

As you look back, you must remember that you have experienced grief for a reason. You are alive. You never have to ask, "What did I do to deserve this?" You didn't do anything and you don't "deserve" the pain you have been through. You are not being punished. There has been no divine court that found you guilty of anything. You have experienced life, you will continue to experience life, and you have made it through the valley of death.

You are reconnected, you are a better, more understanding person than you have ever been, and the most compelling reason for your success is that you never lost your faith.

Your faith is your citadel. Nothing can be accomplished without faith.

I Am Not Gone

I feel your sorrow,
And appreciate your prayers.
When you are lonely
Know that I am nearby for you.
While I'm no longer on earth,
I'm in a new place—
A place too beautiful to describe.
It's a place of peace, comfort, and love,
A place so warm and wonderful
It defies imagination.
I am well cared-for,
And I am preparing a place for you.
While you are sad now,
You will grow in strength.
You can turn to me in prayer—please do.
You can continue to love me.

I will watch over you—though for now
You will not be able to see or touch me.
God has called me home
To meet family, friends,
And those who have gone before us.
You are still on earth
And meant to be there for now.
You will grieve; it isn't easy.
Death is always sad,
But believe that it's only a passing part of life,
And someday soon we'll be reunited
To be all that we can be
With God and our loved ones.
Amen.